Cost-Effectiveness in the Nonprofit Sector

Cost-Effectiveness in the Nonprofit Sector

Methods and Examples from Leading Organizations

Edited by Gerald L. Schmaedick

under the auspices of TechnoServe, Inc.

Q

Quorum Books
Westport, Connecticut • London

Library of Congress Cataloging-in-Publication Data

Cost-effectiveness in the nonprofit sector : methods and examples from
  leading organizations / edited by Gerald L. Schmaedick ; under the
  auspices of TechnoServe.
    p.   cm.
  "Papers presented at the National Workshop on Cost-Effectiveness
in the Nonprofit Sector . . . Stanford University, June 27 & 28,
1991"—Pref.
  Includes bibliographical references and index.
  ISBN 0-89930-627-6 (alk. paper)
  1. Corporations, Nonprofit—Finance—Congresses. 2. Corporations,
Nonprofit—Cost effectiveness—Congresses. 3. Medical care, Cost
of—Congresses. 4. Health facilities—Finance—Congresses.
5. Technical assistance—Congresses. I. Schmaedick, Gerald L.
II. TECHNOSERVE (Organization)
HG4027.65.C67   1993
658.15'52—dc20   92-1746

British Library Cataloguing in Publication Data is available.

Library of Congress Catalog Card Number: 92-1746
ISBN: 0-89930-627-6

First published in 1993

Quorum Books, 88 Post Road West, Westport, CT 06881
An imprint of Greenwood Publishing Group, Inc.

Printed in the United States of America

The paper used in this book complies with the
Permanent Paper Standard issued by the National
Information Standards Organization (Z39.48-1984).

10 9 8 7 6 5 4 3 2 1

Dedicated to

Tom Giddings and Shep Wheeler

Colleagues who, by their lives, taught
us a lot about cost-effectiveness

Contents

Tables and Figures

FIGURES

Preface

The content of this book is drawn principally from papers presented at the National Workshop on Cost-Effectiveness in the Nonprofit Sector. This workshop took place at Stanford University, June 27 and 28, 1991. It was organized by TechnoServe and the Public Management Program of Stanford University. All the chapters, except Chapter 4, reproduce the material presented by the authors at the workshop. Chapter 4 has been added because of its exceptionally clear and articulate statement on the need for cost-effectiveness analysis. The authors of this chapter also provide an unusually persuasive explanation of how to accomplish cost-effectiveness analysis in spite of all the often cited obstacles and limitations. Its application goes far beyond the health sector for which it was originally written.

The origins of the book, however, go beyond the workshop. In the mid-1980s TechnoServe began searching for a way to evaluate the cost-effectiveness of its assistance to groups of subsistence farmers in developing countries. This search led to the development of a methodology which TechnoServe published in 1989 as part of its Findings series. It was titled *Measuring Our Impact: Determining Cost-Effectiveness of Non-Governmental Organization Development Projects*. The appearance of *Measuring Our Impact* gave rise to much discussion within the nonprofit community, especially among those involved in international development.

Encouraged by the widespread interest in the subject, TechnoServe decided to organize a workshop on cost-effectiveness in the nonprofit sector. The focus was to be a practical one. We wanted to provide workshop participants with concrete tools—tools tailored to their own fields, from assisting the homeless to running a museum—with which to evaluate the cost-effectiveness of their activities. To this end, many organizations submitted their methodologies. Again, we were encouraged by the degree of activity and interest this indicated. We decided to include cases from both domestic and internationally oriented nonprofit organizations. The cases presented in this book are those that were presented at the Workshop.

Let me say a word about the TechnoServe case, Chapter 7. The content of this chapter is largely the same as that in *Measuring Our Impact*. I have had the benefit, however, of analyzing all the comments that have been received since it was first published and to integrate lessons learned at the workshop. I have also consulted with several experts in the field of cost-effectiveness and benefit-cost analysis. This has led to several changes which I believe improve the methodology presented. TechnoServe is currently in the process of evaluating these changes and integrating them into its routine project development and follow-up procedures.

This book is, then, the product of a long effort to which many people and organizations contributed. TechnoServe believes that it will help advance the use of cost-effectiveness analysis among nonprofit organizations. This, in turn, will permit these organizations to reach more people with greater benefits at a lower cost. If this is accomplished even in a small way, our efforts will have been truly cost-effective.

Acknowledgments

TechnoServe owes a large debt of gratitude, first and foremost, to the contributors who, without compensation, agreed to reproduce their papers from the National Workshop on Cost-Effectiveness in the Nonprofit Sector in manuscript form for this book. Their contributions to the workshop and to this volume have been indispensable. Their patience throughout the editing process has been greatly appreciated.

The book, of course, would not have been possible without the workshop, and for that we thank, first of all, Peter Reiling and Chris Wrona Giallongo who, with the assistance of Rebecca P. Stewart, worked tirelessly to help make the workshop a great success. The workshop would also not have been possible without the valuable support of our host, Prof. James Thompson, Director of the Public Management Program at the Stanford Graduate School of Business, and our other sponsors, The Independent Sector, and the Support Center of San Francisco. The ever necessary financial support for the workshop came from The James Irvine Foundation, The David and Lucile Packard Foundation, American Express Philanthropic Program, and The Peninsula Community Foundation. To all of these we are very grateful.

As editor of this book I have numerous people and organizations to thank. This is especially true since I assumed responsibility as editor after the workshop had been completed and many of the contributors had already submitted their manuscripts. Peter Reiling and Chris Wrona-Giallongo are to be thanked again for laying the groundwork for this book. Rebecca P. Stewart has been tireless and indispensable in formatting and editing the numerous drafts of this volume. Her efforts are evident on every page. Special thanks are also due Barkley Calkins, James Herne, Barbara Magner, Steve Londner, and Andrea Luery for their valuable comments on my early drafts of Chapter 1.

For the revisions and improvement on the TechnoServe methodology presented in Chapter 7, I am grateful to Dr. J. Price Gittinger, Dr. William Ward, Dr. Peter Kilby, and Dr. J. D. Von Pischke. All of them dedicated more time than one could expect, reviewing and commenting on our work. It is surely better for it.

No list of acknowledgments would be complete without making special note of the indispensable contribution to this effort of TechnoServe's president and founder, Edward P. Bullard. From the very beginning, it was Ed who insisted that TechnoServe must have a way to measure its impact on the people we serve and a way to report to donors on the cost-effectiveness of our efforts. His insistence that we not give up, even when the task seemed technically and operationally overwhelming, has kept this project alive and well at TechnoServe. Without this kind of unequivocal support, the project would have died long ago.

There are others who have helped at various times during the seven years that this project has been under way at TechnoServe. Failure to mention them all individually should not be interpreted as lack of gratitude, but rather as an indication that this has really been an organizationwide effort. I, of course, assume responsibility for the quality and content of the final product.

A Few Words about TechnoServe

TechnoServe is a private, nonsectarian, nonprofit international development agency founded in 1968. Its goal is to improve the long-term economic and social well-being of low-income, rural people in developing countries through a process of enterprise development. Specifically, TechnoServe fosters the establishment and growth of small- to medium-scale, community-based, agricultural enterprises. TechnoServe does this through an integrated approach—assisting rural communities directly by providing technical assistance and training, and indirectly by providing similar services to various local development institutions.

TechnoServe has offices in twelve countries of Africa, Latin America, and Central Europe. Each is staffed primarily by local professionals. TechnoServe's funding comes from foundations, corporations, religious organizations, individuals, host-country institutions, international private voluntary organizations, and bilateral and multilateral governmental organizations, including the U.S. Agency for International Development.

A Few Words about TechnoServe

Cost-
Effectiveness
in the
Nonprofit Sector

1

Introduction: Do Nonprofit Organizations Need Cost-Effectiveness Analysis?

Gerald L. Schmaedick, *TechnoServe, Inc.*

INTRODUCTION

When people in need ask for help, Americans have always responded generously. This generous spirit of giving is what supports the numerous nonprofit organizations in our society. It is a remarkable tradition which is unparalleled in other countries. But this tradition is threatened. News of mismanagement, abuse, and scandal at the highest levels of some of our most respected nonprofit organizations has shaken the public's confidence. It is urgent that nonprofit organizations demonstrate that they are using the donations they receive as the donors intended. Donors will quit giving or find other channels unless they are confident that their donations are being effectively used.

This danger occurs at a time when the nonprofit community is larger and more influential than ever before. Many of the most daunting challenges facing society today are in the hands of nonprofit organizations. Whether it is preserving and displaying precious works of art, sheltering the homeless, combating AIDS, or comforting victims dying from it, our society has opted to entrust these causes to nonprofit organizations. In the international arena, some nonprofit development agencies fight starvation, while others teach subsistence farmers how to become successful commercial farmers. These nonprofit organizations have become indispensable institutions in our society. They nurture our highest aspirations and grapple with our most vexing problems.

In his book *Managing the Non-Profit Organization*, Peter Drucker, commenting on the dramatic increase in importance of the nonprofit sector, says, "We now realize that it is central to the quality of life in America, central to citizenship, and indeed carries the values of American society and of the American tradition" (Drucker, p. xiii). In addition to their strategic importance in our society, the nonprofits have taken on enormous economic importance.

The aggregate value of nonprofit activity reached a total of $389.1 billion in 1990, as indicated in the Table 1.1. This represents 7.1 percent of our gross

Table 1.1
Key Statistics

	1977	1990
Organizations	739,000	983,000
Employees	5,519,500	8,652,300
Percentage of total U.S. employment	5.3%	6.3%
Employee earnings	$46,700,000,000	$156,200,000,000
Percentage of total earnings of U.S. workers	3.9%	4.8%
Volunteers	3,271,000	5,784,000
Operating expenditures[1]	$102,700,000,000	$389,100,000
Adjusted for inflation (1982 dollars)	$162,400,000,000	$263,300,000,000
Per capita	$466	$1,548
Per capita, adjusted for inflation	$737	$1,047
Percentage of U.S. service economy	17.6%	19.6%
Percentage of gross national product	5.2%	7.1%

[1] Figures are for all nonprofits, whereas other figures in the table cover only organizations exempt under Sections 501(c)(3) and 501(c)(4) of the U.S. Tax Code, plus churches.

Source: Reprinted, with permission of *The Chronicle of Philanthropy*, from issue dated January 28, 1992, page 24.

national product and almost 20 percent of the entire service sector of our economy. It exceeds the gross national product of such countries as China ($350 billion) and Brazil ($313 billion). The nonprofit sector employs 8.6 million people. When volunteer employees are added, the sector accounts for 10.4 percent of total employment in the United States. Since 1977, the rate of growth of employment has been more rapid in the nonprofit sector than in either the government or the business sector (Greene, Table 1).

Even before the abuses mentioned earlier occurred, upgrading management was a priority of nonprofit organizations. Managers and boards of directors have been grappling with the increased size and complexity of their organizations. Their focus has been not only on improving overall management, but also on using resources as effectively as possible. As public-sector budgets are cut, the pressure on nonprofits to get more out of each dollar has increased dramatically. Their boards of directors and donors want to know how much benefit they are getting for the dollars spent. In short, they have been looking for a way to measure their cost-effectiveness. The simple assumption that they are "doing good" is not enough.

Recognition of the need for a way to measure cost-effectiveness in nonprofit organizations is what led to this book. The thesis of this book is that cost-effectiveness analysis is a clear necessity for responsible nonprofit management. The examples contained here reveal that many nonprofits are already using various forms of cost-effectiveness analysis. They demonstrate that it is practical and that the rigor involved will improve the organization's internal effectiveness and efficiency and will enhance the organization's external image.

WHAT IS "COST-EFFECTIVENESS"?

This book outlines an approach to increasing the effective use of resources in nonprofit organizations. Many issues—for example, fundraising, strategic planning, and financial management—are related to the overall successful management of nonprofits. While these issues have been and will continue to be the subject of much discussion and literature, this book has a narrower focus: to discuss and illustrate ways nonprofit organizations can become more cost-effective. But just what is cost-effectiveness?

In the 1983 edition of *Webster's Collegiate Dictionary*, "cost-effective" is defined as "economical in terms of tangible benefits produced by money spent" and goes on to give this illustration of its use: "cost-effective measures to combat poverty." During the past decade or more there has been a notable surge in demand that programs be cost-effective. The term did not even appear in the 1963 edition of *Webster's Dictionary*. The origin of the term is a technical one. "Cost-effectiveness analysis" is the name given to a specific analytical tool or methodology used to measure how effectively resources are being utilized—that is, what results are obtained for each unit of input cost. Cost-effectiveness analysis, thus, is a close cousin of cost-benefit analysis. In this book, however, cost-effectiveness analysis is used in the broader, generic sense, which has become the more common usage. When this is not the use intended, it will be noted that the narrower meaning is to be understood.

Each of the chapters that follows illustrates how one organization is striving for a more cost-effective use of its resources. Each utilizes different techniques and methodologies, but they all are searching for the same result: greater benefits, both qualitatively and quantitatively, at the lowest possible cost per unit of benefit (however defined).

In none of cases presented does this search depend *only* on applying a simple formula. Each organization is implementing, to a greater or lesser extent, management procedures that permit comparison of the results achieved to the costs incurred. This is cost-effectiveness analysis (CEA) in the more general sense, as used in this chapter. It is a process that varies greatly from one organization to another, but that has certain common principles and ingredients for all. This process is part of their routine management practices.

What are these common principles and generally recognizable ingredients? The rest of this chapter discusses them, and each chapter illustrates them in the context of different kinds of organizations. However, all of these organizations use an approach that fits the following definition of CEA: *A rigorous system which tracks the costs of an activity or program and records the results, or at least indicators of results, then compares the two in terms that permit an evaluation of whether the results justify the costs.* From this definition it is clear that the use of CEA in this book is not tied to a single, narrowly defined methodology or formula. Rather, the organizations represented take the popular concept of cost-effectiveness as found in *Webster's Collegiate Dictionary* and put it into the context of the management process. What does a nonprofit organization have to do to ensure that it is managing cost-effectively? What are the ingredients of cost-effective management?

The analytical content of CEA is contained in the method of tracking the project that permits and facilitates a rigorous comparison of results and costs. Evaluating whether the results justify the costs will always be an act of judgment. There is no practical formula or technique that produces measurements so conclusive as to eliminate the need for judgment. Not every evaluator will reach the same conclusion from the data produced by the analysis. But if the analysis is done well, every evaluator's conclusion will be better because of it.

Much can be learned from the experience of nonprofits (NPs) that have designed and implemented CEA systems. The chapters of this book are excellent illustrations of good, successful attempts to measure organizational cost-effectiveness. Two important conclusions can be reached from all of this. First, NPs can carry out useful cost-effectiveness analyses. In spite of technical limitations, it is possible to design a system that gives meaningful results and can be carried out within the budget and personnel constraints faced by most NPs. Second, we can also learn what the principles are for a good CEA system. That is, these chapters reveal common ingredients of successful CEA systems.

NONPROFITS CAN DO COST-EFFECTIVENESS ANALYSIS

"Is CEA possible for my organization?" This was one of the most important questions on the mind of those in attendance at the National Workshop on Cost-Effectiveness in the Nonprofit Sector. Cook's chapter—"Are We Barking up the Wrong Tree?"—provides a very informative, as well as entertaining, discussion on the pros and cons of doing cost-effectiveness analysis at all. If you are already convinced that NPs can and should do CEA, read this chapter first. After a lively recital of the popular opinions against CEA, Cook concludes that

the reality regarding *external* uses of information about the cost-effectiveness of nonprofits is a disgrace. Outside the boundaries of a single nonprofit organization, information about cost-effectiveness is virtually never used objectively or competently. Theoretically, the most important external use of such information is to enable effective allocation of resources to specific organizations and methods. But such factors as influence, loyalty, fund-raising skill, and fund-raising expenditure are much more significant determinants of where dollars go in our sector. For the most part, information about what works—or which organizations work—makes little or no difference in determining how resources are allocated by external sources to nonprofit organizations. So why bother? [See the section entitled "The Case against Measuring 'Cost-Effectiveness'."]

It is clearly an argument that cannot be discarded easily. Even if CEA can help the organization, internally as Cook affirms earlier, is it really worth it? In the chapters by Cohen Pine (see the section entitled "How Cost-Effective Is Analyzing Cost-Effectiveness?") and Johnston Nicholson and Weiss (see the section entitled "Cost-Effectiveness of Conducting Cost-Effectiveness Analysis"), each author specifically addresses the question of the cost-effectiveness of their own CEA efforts.

In one form or another all the authors struggle with this question. However, if the question is broken down into the logical components suggested by the definition of CEA given above, some answers emerge.

- Can NPs gather data on their costs and results?
- Should the relationship between costs and results be analyzed?
- Should the conclusions reached inform policy and management decisions of the organization?

The evidence contained in the chapters that follow seems to answer all these questions with a resounding "Yes." In fact, in light of the magnitude and importance of the work NPs are doing, failing to do so would not seem to be an option. After recognizing that CEA in the health sector must depend on uncertain data and subjective values, Weinstein and Stason, in their see chapter entitled "Foundations of Cost-Effectiveness Analysis," conclude, "Nevertheless, resource-allocation decisions do have to be made, and the choice is often between relying upon a responsible analysis with all its imperfections, and no analysis at all. The former, in these times of increasingly complex decisions, difficult trade-offs, and limited resources, is by far the preferred choice." (See the section entitled "Conclusions on the Value and Application of Cost-Effectiveness Analysis in Health Care.")

The conclusion that one reaches is that CEA is a clear necessity for responsible nonprofit management. While it is easy to agree with this conclusion, carrying the principle into practice is a lot more difficult.

THE PRINCIPLES OF GOOD COST-EFFECTIVENESS ANALYSIS

Using the definition of CEA discussed above as a basis, each organization can design its own procedures for analyzing its cost- effectiveness. Five principles should be followed to ensure that the design of the CEA system gives the organization the impact on its cost-effectiveness that it is seeking:

1. Develop and follow a clearly stated, well-focused mission statement, which sets out the goal of the organization or activity.

2. Design and implement a system for recording and analyzing all the costs of the inputs used to achieve specific results. As far as possible costs should be expressed in monetary terms.

3. Design and implement a system for recording results (or indicators of results)—positive and negative, quantifiable and non-quantifiable, expected and unexpected.

4. Design and implement a system that compares results to costs and culminates in a judgment regarding the symmetry between costs and results.

5. Follow a routine procedure in which the board and management use CEA results in setting policy and establishing budgets for the organization.

The cases presented in this book give ample evidence that very different organizations can devise successful CEA systems. A careful study of these cases also suggests that the principles proposed here are those that should form the basis of any good CEA system. All of the cases follow these five principles—not all to the same degree, but sufficiently to encourage cost-effectiveness within the organization and give management a means to check progress toward becoming more cost-effective.

In the sections that follow, each of the principles is discussed and illustrations of their application from subsequent chapters are presented.

Principle One: The Mission Statement

If an organization is to be cost-effective, it must first know what it is trying to achieve. It is impossible to carry out good CEA without a clearly state, well-focused mission statement. The mission statement gives the framework within which the goals of the organization or activity are set. These goals permit the definition of bench marks to be achieved in the pursuit of the goals. The CEA system tracks costs related to the achievement of the goals and records indicators that tell when and if the bench marks have been met. It all depends on the mission statement. Peter Drucker says it very eloquently:

One starts with the mission, and that is exceedingly important. . . . The mission is something that transcends today, but guides today, informs today. The moment we lose sight of the mission, we waste resources. From the mission, one goes to very concrete goals. Only when a nonprofit's key performance areas are defined can it really set goals. Only then can the nonprofit ask: "Are we doing what we are supposed to be doing? Is it still the right activity? Does it still serve a need?" And, above all, "Do we still produce results that are sufficiently outstanding, sufficiently different for us to justify putting our talents to use in that area?" (Drucker, p. 141)

One could easily paraphrase this last question as "Do we still produce *cost-effective* results?"

All of the organizations represented in this volume illustrate the importance of a well-defined mission as a starting point for an effective CEA system. Two, however, demonstrate this particularly well. Assessing the cost-effectiveness of an art gallery is no doubt one of the most abstract, intangible, impossible-to-quantify challenges in the application of CEA. Throughout her chapter, National Gallery of Art Administrator Anne Evans constantly returns to one theme, "The Gallery is . . . relentlessly true to its mission." (See the section entitled "Promoting Cost-Effectiveness.") Obedience to its mission is the cardinal rule of the CEA system used by the National Gallery of Art. In an environment where results are manifested in such abstract, intangible ways, the mission must play an even more important role in a CEA system.

The case of The Nature Conservancy, presented by Halperin, Williams, and Stewart is the other example. It, too, relies in a special way on its mission statement. The CEA system of The Nature Conservancy is an integral part of its overall strategic planning and management procedures. This is summed up in the conclusion to Chapter 6. "The Nature Conservancy's cyclical approach to cost-effectiveness, therefore, is woven throughout its operational procedures. It does not depend on one or two specific tools applied periodically to measure cost-effectiveness. Rather, the methodology is focused on a continuous effort to carry the mission of the Conservancy throughout all aspects of the organization. By rating and evaluating each portion of the strategic plan, annual plan, budget, and, finally internal feedback mechanisms, cost-effectiveness occurs within each program." (See the section entitled "Conclusion.")

The concept of "mission" is important to CEA for another reason. It defines the focus of the analysis. Often an organization wishes to analyze the cost-effectiveness of one component of its program, not the entire program. Educational institutions provide a good example. As Balderston points out in Chapter 5, universities have at least three functions: instruction, research, and community service (see the section entitled "Activity Analysis of Higher Education"). CEA could be carried out on any one of these components and even on their subcomponents (e.g., agricultural research). The mission statement or "activity" statement provides limits for the analysis. This is very important in deciding what costs to include in the estimation of the cost of the activity or program. Similarly, it helps to decide what benefits can be included. For example, the TechnoServe CEA system focuses only on the agricultural enterprise being assisted. TechnoServe's mission is to "improve the economic and social well-being of low-income farmers" by teaching them to make their farm enterprises profitable. The costs included in the CEA are TechnoServe's costs of assisting the farmers' enterprise. The quantifiable benefits are the financial gains of the farmers and their enterprise. The non-quantifiable benefits, which are also included in the CEA system, include such things as the improved leadership ability of the farmers and the increased participation of women. All costs and benefits are defined in terms of the unit identified in the mission statement (i.e., the enterprise).

The most ambitious CEA systems attempt to evaluate the impact of a given program on society as a whole. Such analysis is implemented when the mission statement is so broad as to require it. While the impact of their program on the entire society may be of interest to many nonprofits, this level of analysis requires substantial resources and a more complex methodology. A more focused partial analysis is often enough to meet the needs of a local nonprofit. Good examples of the two approaches are found in the chapters by Johnston Nicholson and Weiss (impact on society) and by Miller Franco (organizational impact).

Principle Two: Tracking and Recording and Analyzing Costs

At first look, compiling a thorough and accurate record of costs appears to be a routine task in the overall CEA process. To a great extent this can be true, but as the analysis gets more sophisticated, pinning down costs can become very complicated. Frequently, it is best to opt for the least complicated alternative in recording costs since the analysis is only as good as its weakest component. If a uniform level of sophistication is not possible with costs, results, and the method of comparison, then the extra time and expense required to record costs will be wasted. In his excellent work *Cost-Effectiveness: A Primer*, Henry M. Levin dedicates an entire chapter to analyzing costs. He points out, for example, that "Although the existence of budgets is universal, the assumption that they will contain all of the cost information that is needed is usually erroneous" (Levin, 1983, p. 50).

Nevertheless, a good accounting system is the first step toward a CEA that is based on a reliable estimate of costs. This is obvious but achieving it is another matter. Since CEA is most useful if the costs of activities that directly impact on the beneficiaries are known, the accounting system has to be good at the lowest levels in the organization, not just at the highest levels where aggregation of data occurs. How much does it actually cost to deliver the meal to the elderly person? What is the cost per student for a tutoring program utilizing other student volunteers? Many accounting systems are not adequate to specify costs at this level of disaggregation. Cohen Pine refers to this kind of problem in her chapter on services for the homeless. However, these problems can usually be overcome if the accounting system gives at least good aggregate costs. The point made earlier is worth repeating. It is better to have some analysis, even if the data are imperfect, than no analysis.

The most important question to be addressed when dealing with costs is, What costs should be included? Are the costs that appear in the accounting books of your organization enough? Do they reflect all of your costs? Do they reflect all of the costs incurred in producing the results you are claiming? If you are estimating the effect of a summer recreation program on teenage crime, should some cost of increased police patrols be factored in also? Balderston addresses this kind of a problem. "Those costs arising within, and processed through, the institution's accounting system are within the boundaries for determination of institutional costs. But some cost analysis necessarily ignores or pierces the institutional boundary." (See the section entitled "Cost Categories and Boundaries.)

Referring again to the mission or activity statement is often necessary to reach the right decision on what costs to include. Weinstein and Stason point out that, for example, analysis of costs of a given health intervention will be different when viewed from the varying perspectives of doctor, hospital, and insurance provider. (See the section entitled "Elements of Cost-Effectiveness Analysis.") They are each concerned about the health of the patient, but see costs attributable to their respective roles differently. A common dichotomy in this regard is between the view of costs and benefits for the society as a whole versus the "managerial" perspective (i.e., how much of the resources under my managerial control did I have to allocate to achieve a particular outcome?) Which of these perspectives you adopt must be clearly stated at the outset of the analysis. Much confusion arises in the implementation of CEA exercises due to lack of clarity on this point.

For example, the methodologies presented in the chapters by TechnoServe, Miller Franco, and Cohen Pine all take the narrower managerial perspective. But Johnston Nicholson and Weiss estimate the savings to society of preventing or delaying teenage pregnancy. They are able to adopt this perspective at virtually no cost beyond the "managerial" cost of doing the study by intelligently drawing on another study to estimate the benefit of a pregnancy avoided. This estimate is then simply multiplied by the number of pregnancies avoided projected in their own study. This is a wonderful example of how CEA can be accomplished at a lower cost than might be expected. The Johnston Nicholson and Weiss study enabled Girls, Inc., to report that its program to reduce adolescent pregnancies helped twenty-two young women avoid the agony of an unwanted pregnancy. The cost of the program was about $34,000, and it saved taxpayers almost six times that much in public expenditures (see Table 3.6).

Principle Three: Recording Results

Perhaps the objection most frequently and most stridently lodged against attempting CEA is that "We know we are serving people. They are better off. We just can't measure our results. What we accomplish is too intangible. It can't be quantified!" The chapters in this book prove that objection to be a straw man. Thoughtful nonprofit managers are finding ways to demonstrate the results of their work and compare them to costs, which have also been carefully recorded. The data on results may be flawed or incomplete. But conscientious studies are producing results that are far better than nothing at all!

The first step is to collect *some* data. A good accounting system is the first step in recording costs. Unfortunately, there is no analogous standardized system for recording results. The diversity of the nonprofit sector makes such standardization impossible. But each nonprofit can gather some data on its own impact. Cook is pretty hard on the nonprofit sector on this. He says, "We do things that pretend to be measurement—we love to promulgate misleading measures." (See the section entitled "No Common Measures of What We Do.") It is possible to collect data on what we are doing—no matter how intangible. The work of Cohen Pine in Chapter 8 is an absolutely ingenious example of what can be done with serious effort and creativity.

Cohen Pine was asked to help design a system to evaluate the cost-effectiveness of the housing and human services program of the Shelter Network of San Mateo County, California. Using a framework based on Maslow's hierarchy of human needs, she defined the desired outcomes of the program in terms of a pyramid model. "Based on this framework, we defined *individual needs* (i.e., Food, Clothing, Education, Self-Esteem, etc.) as the 'building blocks' of the pyramid. We defined *human needs* as the combined instrumental, stabilization, and emotional needs shown in the Pyramid Model. We then defined the desired outcome of Shelter Network's programs as increasing the degree to which participants' *human needs* are met over time." (See the section entitled "Description.")

Surveys were used to permit participants to assess their own progress up the pyramid. There will always be questions about technical aspects of this kind of ad hoc generation of analytical methodologies. But at least the organization now has a system for collecting data on its results and a framework within which to use the data. Weinstein and Stason make a clear case for using the "best available evidence," rather then waiting for scientifically valid proof (see the section entitled "General Analytic Approaches"). The contributions to this book are rich in examples of thoughtful ways to identify indicators of impact and systems for collecting them. In particular, Miller Franco's chapter on health and Halperin, Williams, and Stewart's chapter on the environment are interesting in addition to the ones already mentioned.

A final note on results. A common weakness among nonprofits today is that they collect data on inputs and present them as evidence of results. For example, an adult literacy program reports a great success because 95 percent of the illiterate population of XYZ region *attended literacy classes*. Chapter 7 on TechnoServe's CEA system cites this problem in the field of international economic development. "Many people in the development field are accustomed to measuring the number of dollars spent, vaccines shipped, loans made, or training hours invested as a sufficient way of estimating the effectiveness of a development project. These factors are signs of progress and can be readily measured. But they do not in themselves reflect development 'output.' By focusing on efforts, we may lose sight of the true objectives of development work: sustainable results." (See the section entitled Introduction.)

Referring again to the mission statement is the best way to see if the indicators selected are really indicators of results. Would the observer of the data truly be able to conclude "mission accomplished" from the data provided? If not, you are probably measuring what Balderston calls "intermediate products" (see the section entitled "Effects, Results, Outputs") or just inputs. It is time to go back to the drawing board and see what kind of data can be collected that will reveal end products (i.e., *results*).

Principle Four: Comparing Results and Costs

If good work has been done in the tracking of costs and the recording of benefits, or indicators of benefits, the process of comparing the two should be relatively simple and straightforward. Nevertheless, it is this part that strikes fear in the hearts of many nonprofit managers and board members.

Let us look more closely at the principle as stated above: Design and implement a system that compares results to costs and that culminates in a judgment regarding the symmetry between costs and results. The key words are "judgment" and "symmetry." Because the data that go into CEA are always imperfect, comparisons of the data must always be carried out with a great deal of judgment. At times, the case may be quite clear from the data alone, but more often the analysis is only an aid to judgment. What Weinstein and Stason say about the use of CEA in the health field is equally true in others. "To be explicit about quality of life, and possible trade-offs between longevity and quality, subjective values are necessarily involved. A useful analysis should serve the important function of incorporating these values into a rational framework for decision making." (See the section entitled "Prerequisites for Useful Cost-Effective Analysis.")

The "rational framework for decision making" is enhanced by the method used to compare results and costs. Many methods can be used, as illustrated by the choices of the authors of the following chapters. Two organizations used the traditional benefit-cost (B-C) analysis formula. The example given by Girls, Inc. (Johnston Nicholson and Weiss) applies only B-C analysis. The other organization, TechnoServe (Bowman et al.), combines the specific formula for cost-effectiveness (C-E) analysis with a rating system in order to incorporate non-quantifiable benefits into its overall CEA system. TechnoServe's methodology does not link the two, but a high C-E ratio combined with a high non-quantifiable benefit rating would strongly indicate a very cost-effective project with significant impact on intangibles. The approach used by these two organizations should be of special interest to organizations that can quantify at least some significant part of their impact.

Three other chapters illustrate how the specific formula for C-E analysis can be used to compare costs and results. The difference between the B-C and the C-E formulas is amply described both in the TechnoServe chapter (see Table 7.1) and in Weinstein and Stason chapter (see the section entitled "General Analytic Approaches"). The distinguishing feature is that B-C analysis requires that both cost and benefits be expressed in monetary terms, while the C-E formula requires that only costs be expressed in monetary terms.

As described in the section on costs above, Cohen Pine uses a "pyramid of needs" to help describe the benefits in her C-E formula. Miller Franco proposes a very useful extension of the C-E formula which she calls "cost-coverage analysis." It compares the costs of various health services or coverages. According to Miller Franco, cost-coverage analysis "concentrates on the intermediate steps that lead to coverage, and it stops short of impact to focus on effective coverage. *Effective coverage* can be defined as the percentage of those people requiring a certain intervention who receive it in a correct and timely manner. Effective coverage is a proxy measure for effectiveness or impact." (See the section entitled "The Cost-Coverage Alternative to Cost-Effectiveness Analysis.")

The chapter by Weinstein and Stason is an exceptionally clear and readable description of how CEA is applicable to the health sector. The lessons of this chapter are widely transferable to other nonprofit sectors. Two other chapters, one on The Nature Conservancy (Halperin, Williams, and Stewart) and the other on the National Gallery of Art (Evans), do not formally make a direct comparison of benefits and costs. However, they describe managerial procedures that involve such comparisons.

What Is Symmetry in Cost versus Benefit Comparisons?

As we all intuitively know, and as the cases presented in this book show, there is no one formula into which we can put the costs and indicators of results from all or even the majority of situations and get a simple answer. Results are often impossible to quantify, let alone estimate in monetary terms. Costs are not always as easy to evaluate as they may seem. So we are left with the task of comparing things that are not very comparable. CEA in the nonprofit sector often requires us to compare the monetary value of certain interventions with their life-altering consequences.

Examples are all too easy to think of—the cost of programs versus their impact on housing the homeless; rehabilitating the substance abuser; providing libraries for children in isolated, depressed areas; extending the life of a cancer victim; and so on. What value can we put on all these things compared to their costs? The CEA methodologies discussed in this chapter can shed light on these choices. They can provide order and logic to the process of comparison and suggest standards by which the choices might be measured. Where possible, the measurements can even be provided to better inform the decision. But in the last analysis most of the time it comes down to a judgment. The choice is not as simple as, "Is the value of the benefit greater than, less than, or equal to its cost?" Rather, we must ask if the relationship between the cost and the benefit seems reasonable. Does the cost seem out of proportion to the benefit? *If reasonable judgement leads to the conclusion that the benefits justify the costs, then there is symmetry.*

If the CEA is good, it should help us see the benefits more clearly and have a firmer, more reliable estimate of costs. And whatever the technique used for the comparison of the two, it should facilitate our judgment. That is the real value of CEA and nonprofit organizations are more likely to accomplish their mission if they use it.

Principle Five: Management Use of CEA Results

Most organizations that do CEA agree that the process used to arrive at the final indicator of cost-effectiveness is more important than the indicator itself. This point is made in most of the chapters included here. Bowman and her colleagues conclude, "In the course of our efforts, we came to appreciate the value of the cost-effectiveness measurement *process* itself. Some TechnoServe employees concluded that the process was ultimately more important than its eventual product. Through structuring the analysis, debating the elements, and assessing the impact that variables have on the end result, our staff learned more about the implications and impact of their projects than the C-E results reflect." (See the section entitled "Analysis of the Method.") The implication of this is that the organization will be "forced" to pay attention to the CEA because the process draws people into contact with it. This will be especially true if the work is done by regular line staff. It also says that if the CEA work is assigned to a special unit, out of the mainstream of the organization, the lessons could be missed by the rest. Another point made in the chapter on TechnoServe is that implementing a CEA system *"requires strong commitment by top management."* (See the section entitled "Lessons Learned.")

In short, in order to ensure optimal utilization of the CEA system within an organization, top management must be behind it, and the system must be part of routine management practices. There is, in fact, a strong case that can be made to convince an organization to observe these principles. The value to the organization internally has already been suggested. Even if data from CEA were never used outside the organization, it has the power to focus attention on fulfilling the mission, on examining costs more carefully, on assessing results, and on demanding data that will otherwise inform management. This is illustrated in the Johnston Nicholson and Weiss chapter, which cites a variety of program changes made possible by the findings of the CEA (see the section entitled "Cost-Effectiveness of Conducting Cost-Effectiveness Analysis"). Similar benefits are reported by Miller Franco. The cost-coverage model she employed enabled managers to detect "where the bottlenecks to coverage are occurring in the coverage determinant hierarchy. Managers can then assess the costs of strategies for improving coverage by estimating the effects." (See the section entitled "Understanding the Effects of Strategies to Improve Coverage on Costs.")

Following the first four principles of good CEA will generate valuable data on costs and results. Even if comparisons suggested in the fourth principle are only tenuous, the data will be informative, and the analysis will inevitably include some interesting suggestions useful to management. The analysis will also be extremely valuable in revealing how the project "fits" in its environment. Are the implicit and explicit assumptions that underlie the project correct and appropriate? Are the goals realistic? Is the mission statement still relevant? Balderston describes the use of CEA to evaluate the year-around operation of the California University system. A costly six-year experiment failed when assumptions of the analysis did not materialize (see section entitled "Budgeted Year-Round Operation of University of California Campuses"). CEA does not always work.   But the problem was surely detected sooner   because the assumptions were known.

The chapter by Weinstein and Stason is emphatic on this point.   "The principal value of formal cost-effectiveness analysis in health care is that it forces one to be explicit about the beliefs and values that underlie allocation decisions.   Opposing points of view can be clarified in terms of specific agreements over assumptions, probability estimates, or value trade-offs." (See the section entitled "Conclusions on the Value and Application of Cost-Effectiveness Analysis in Health Care.") This is not only true in the health sector; this is applicable to the nonprofit sector as a whole.

Of course, the hope is that CEA will generate data that are useful externally as well.   The link between the results and the costs incurred to obtain them is of great interest to all outside observers of nonprofits. This is particularly true in the case of donors. In the initial stages of installing a CEA system, the results obtained may not be appropriate for donor use. Data may be incomplete and out of context.   However, until the system is refined enough to produce information useful to donors, one of the greatest benefits of the CEA system will be missed.

WHAT TO LOOK FOR IN THE CHAPTERS THAT FOLLOW

This chapter began by describing the importance and magnitude of the nonprofit sector.   Society has entrusted many of its greatest challenges to this sector.   Every year the public gives the sector billions of dollars.   Nonprofit organizations have a responsibility to use these resources to generate the maximum benefits possible for the dollars spent; that is, they have a responsibility to manage their resources *cost-effectively*.   But what constitutes cost-effective management? Drawing on the experiences described in this book and on the author's own experience, a definition of cost-effectiveness analysis was proposed.   Based on this definition, five principles of cost-effective management were presented. The application of these principles was illustrated by examples from the chapters that follow.

But each chapter has its own contribution to make to answering the question we started out with: Do nonprofit organizations need cost-effectiveness analysis? Each chapter offers a different methodology for dealing with the specific problems of implementing CEA. Each chapter illustrates a different level of rigor in applying the five principles of CEA. It is in the richness of this detail that the best answer to our original question is found.

REFERENCES

Anandarup, Ray. *Cost-Benefit Analysis: Issues and Methodologies*. Baltimore: Publications for the World Bank by Johns Hopkins University Press, 1984.

Austin, Michael J., and Gary Cox. Evaluating Your Agency's Programs. Beverly Hills, Calif.: Sage Publications, 1982.

Cameron, Kim S., and David A. Whetten, eds. *Organizational Effectiveness: A Comparison of Multiple Models*. New York: Academic Press, 1983.

Carter, Reginald K. *The Accountable Agency*. Beverly Hills, Calif.: Sage Publications, 1983.

Catterall, J. S., ed. *Economic Evaluation of Public Programs*. New Directions for Program Evaluation, no.26. San Francisco: Jossey-Bass, 1985.

Cooke, Thomas J., ed. "Evaluation Research in International Development." *Evaluation Review: A Journal of Applied Social Research* 13 (June 1989): 206-319.

Coombs, Philip H., and Jacques Hallack. *Cost Analysis in Education: A Tool for Policy and Planning*. Baltimore: Publications for the World Bank by Johns Hopkins University Press, 1987.

Drucker, Peter F. *Managing the Non-Profit Organization*. New York: Harper Collins, 1990.

Freeman, Howard E., Peter H. Rossi and Sonia R. Wright. *Evaluating Social Projects in Developing Countries*. Paris: Development Centre of the Organisation for Economic Co-operation and Development, 1979.

Gittinger, J. Price. *Economic Analysis of Agricultural Projects*. Baltimore: Johns Hopkins University Press, 1982.

Gramlich, E. *Benefit-Cost Analysis of Government Programs*. Englewood Cliffs, N.J.: Prentice-Hall, 1981.

Greene, Stephen G. "The Non-Profit World: a Statistical Portrait." *The Chronicle of Philanthropy* 28 (January 1992): 24.

Gross, Kristin A. "Peter Drucker Wants to Move Charities 'From Good Intentions to Effectiveness'." *The Chronicle of Philanthropy* 13 (June 1989): A1+.

Heng-Kang, Sang. *Project Evaluation: Techniques and Practices for Developing Countries*. New York: Wilson Press, 1988.

Kilby, Peter, and David D'Zmura. *Searching for Benefits*. AID Special Study no. 28. Washington D,C.: Agency for International Development, 1985.

Layard, Richard, ed. *Cost-Benefit Analysis*. Baltimore: Penguin Books, 1972.

Levin, Henry M. "Cost-Effectiveness Analysis in Evaluation Research." In *Handbook of Evaluation Research*. Vol. 2. Beverly Hills, Calif.: Sage Publications, 1975.

Levin, Henry M. *Cost Effectiveness: A Primer*. Beverly Hills, Calif.: Sage Publications, 1983.

Little, Ian M.D., and James A. Mirrlees. *Manual of Industrial Project Analysis in Developing Countries*. Vol. 2. Paris: Development Centre of the Organisation for Economic Co-operation and Development, 1968.

Mikeseii, Raymond F. "Depletable Resources: Discounting and Intergenerational Equity." *Resources Policy: The International Journal of Minerals Policy and Economics* 15 (December 1983): 292-96.

Pearce, David R. *Cost-Benefit Analysis*. New York: St. Martin's, 1983.

Prosavac, Emil J., and Raymond G. Carey. *Program Evaluation: Methods and Case Studies*. Englewood Cliffs, N.J.: Prentice-Hall, 1980.

Reynolds, Jack, and K. Celeste Gaspari. *Cost Effectiveness Analysis*. Operations Research Methods, no.2. Bethesda, Md.: Pricor, 1988.

Sechrest, Lee, and William H. Yeaton. "Assessing the Effectiveness of Social Programs: Methodological and Conceptual Issues." In *New Directions for Program Evaluation: Assessing and Interpreting Outcomes*. Vol.9. San Francisco: Jossey-Bass, 1981. Reprinted in *Evaluation Studies Review Annual*. Vol.7. Edited by Ernest House, Sandra Mathison, James Pearsol, and Hallie Preskill, Beverly Hills, Calif.: Sage Publications, 1982. 151-65.

Ward, William A., and Barry J. Deren. *The Economics of Project Analysis*. Washington, D.C.: The World Bank, 1991.

Wortman, Paul M. "Cost Effectiveness: A Review." *Evaluation Studies Review*. Vol.9. Edited by Ross F. Conner, David G. Altman, and Christine Jackson, (1984): 308-22.

Yates, Brian T. "Cost-Effectiveness Analysis and Cost-Benefit Analysis: An Introduction." *Behavioral Assessment*. Vol.7. Reprinted in *Evaluation Studies Review Annual*. Vol.11. Edited by David S. Cadray, and Mark Lipsey, Beverly Hills, Calif.: Sage Publications, 1986. 314-42.

2

Cost-Effectiveness and the Arts

Anne B. Evans, *National Gallery of Art*

INTRODUCTION

So many of you here today are involved in meeting the basic human needs of clothing, shelter, and health services. It is strange, therefore, to shift gears to think of the principles of cost-effectiveness as applied to an art museum. Art museums, by their nature, are involved more with the human spirit than with human survival, but we view our role as nonetheless important in enriching the lives of both the general public and scholars.

It is our mission at the National Gallery of Art to preserve the nation's collection of irreplaceable works of art and to present it to the public in a manner that is enlightening, enriching, and educational. We pursue programs of collecting, conservation, education, and scholarship, exhibiting works and lending works to other institutions. We educate the public through one-on-one contact, through materials sent to schools and teachers, through our publishing program, and with reproductions of the fabulous works of art in our collections. We conserve the works, and we pursue scientific investigation into ever better methods of conservation. In short, we see the National Gallery of Art as having the responsibility to set standards for quality for the museum field nationally and internationally.

It is important to know that the National Gallery of Art been around only 50 years. The Gallery was opened in 1941 with the gift of its beautiful West Building by Andrew W. Mellon, who also gave one of the major collections of all time of great works of art. At the time of his gift, the conditions were set in motion that are still in place today—that is, that all works of art would be obtained through private donations, but that the U.S. government would pay for operating costs in perpetuity.

As the administrator of the National Gallery of Art, I am responsible for the security of the collection, as well as for all the day-to-day operations of the Gallery, which include the running of two major monumental buildings that are works of art themselves, encompassing 1.2 million square feet of space. I also bear responsibility for most of the staff functions at the Gallery, the Gallery's publications sales business, and its concessionaire arrangements with food service and recorded tour contractors. The administrator position entails the management of two-thirds of the Gallery's staff (670 of a staff of 1,000) a federal operating budget of over $30 million, and a capital budget of approximately $6 million per year.

The Gallery is free to the public and its annual visitation has ranged in recent years between 5 and 7 million people, which makes it the most well attended art museum in the world. The character of the institution also is quite distinctive. The Gallery has had only three directors in its history. The third, J. Carter Brown, is an M.B.A. and an art history scholar in his own right. At fifty-six years of age, he has had 30 years of experience at the National Gallery and is known for his fantastic eye, his energy, and his relentless pursuit of quality. As Carter has said, "Beauty is our business." The Gallery is known for its entrepreneurial approach; yet, at the same time, the Gallery feels the influence of its federal funding through the regulations that control its procurement practices, its personnel hiring and management practices, and its budget process, which requires that budgets be submitted two years in advance.

In addition to Carter Brown, there are six executive officers who serve as the management group for the Gallery. As administrator, I am one of that group. Prior to coming to the Gallery, I had almost ten years of experience in the private sector. From my vantage point, there are both striking similarities and striking differences between how the National Gallery of Art addresses issues regarding the cost-effectiveness of its efforts and how the private sector addresses similar questions. Let me divide my comments from this point on, therefore, into two categories, speaking first about those areas of greatest similarity to private-sector management and concluding with those most specific to the world of museums.

SIMILARITIES TO THE PRIVATE SECTOR

Many problems and decisions in the museum environment lend themselves to traditional analytical approaches. Payback analysis, rate-of-return analysis, and cost-benefit analysis are all useful when looking at energy management investments, when deciding if we should have an internal cashroom for our publication operations instead of purchasing those services from our bank, and when determining whether we should begin a broad membership program or continue to have more selective donor development efforts. In our publication sales operation, we care about inventory turns and about the trend of sales and profit-per-visitor. We watch our sales and profit per square foot and try to make the most effective and efficient use of our staff. When we consider whether to locate certain functions off-site, we consider both long-term and short-term costs in a fashion that is very similar to the analysis that a private sector institution would pursue.

Because 73 percent of the cost of running the National Gallery is tied up in personnel compensation, the productivity of our staff is a major concern. Among the staff supporting the programs of an institution like the National Gallery are the professional fund-raisers in the corporate relations office. Their efforts are, in many ways, the easiest to evaluate through traditional methods. We take note of the dollars that they are able to raise through a given approach, and we evaluate the productivity of one development effort versus another, as well as the "hit-rate" we achieve in our requests for funds. This particular aspect of our fundraising allows us a clear-eyed way to judge the cost effectiveness of development programs. Similarly, with our procurement and personnel staffs, we are able to establish time standards for handling their work load and are able to document the dollars saved through our efforts to obtain competition in contracting.

In other supporting areas, decisions about cost-effectiveness are made according to the level of expected improvement in the service of one internal department to another. For example, we recently installed an automated maintenance management system designed to track work-order requests given to our facilities management group and to ensure that materials are available for preventative maintenance projects at the time those projects are to be accomplished. Considerable investment was made in this system, but we anticipated fewer lost requests and greater ease in following up on requests and tracking work load, as well as improved productivity of our staff of over 150 operations and maintenance employees.

Not all cost-effectiveness decisions are made in pure dollars-and-cents terms, however. Quality and performance can be highly visible in other ways in a museum, much as they are in many service businesses. With our maintenance staff, for example, much of their performance can be measured by the old principle "what you see is what you get." The beauty of the buildings and their cleanliness speak for themselves and provide the setting for the superb works of art. Any inattention to the maintenance of our public spaces is easily seen because it creates such a glaring contrast to the beauty of the works of art on the walls. We can easily compare the relative costs and benefits of one cleaning approach versus those of another.

However, we also spend considerable energy paying attention to what the public does not see. Climate control, the maintenance of a consistent temperature and humidity, is critical to the long-term survival of the works of art in our collection. Today, an extremely people-intensive approach is taken at the National Gallery to ensuring that this climate is controlled because we currently lack an automated building system. Analyses we have done show us that a more cost-effective approach to maintaining the climate does exist, and we are currently switching over to an automated building management system.

In some cases, the nonprofit and private sectors have an equally difficult time determining the cost-effectiveness of their efforts. For example, when making some technology-related decisions, the National Gallery of Art faces challenges very similar to those faced by many technology-intensive businesses. Currently, we are examining the potential uses of digital imaging technology. Technology is emerging that enables us to reproduce a work of art from the Gallery's collection at a high enough level of quality that we are extremely interested in the potential for public dissemination and scholarly study of digitized images. In an institution where presentation of the highest-quality image and public art education are at the heart of our mission, one can argue that we must invest to the limit of the resources we have available to spend in that kind of an endeavor. But determining the most cost-effective way to approach a new technology is extremely difficult because of uncertainty as to how that technology will evolve. In this respect, I believe the private sector has no easier time than do we in the nonprofit sector. The best we can do is keep remembering why we are here—what our mission is—and keep testing the usefulness of the new technologies in helping us achieve our end goals.

There are other uses for technology in our business that are a little easier to manage. For example, we are pursuing the use of computer-aided design (CAD) to ease and speed the production of exhibition space designs. It is clear that the process a designer must go through in producing drawings that contractors can use to construct an exhibition space is considerably more efficient if the base drawings on which those details will be drawn already exist in a computer. Yet we struggle to come up with the investment dollars required to get us to that point. Clearly, one has to make such choices based on the long-term, as well as the short-term, impact of such an investment. For us, we believe that the anticipated staff time saved over the long haul will be worth the considerable up-front investment that we are making, not only in the funds needed to purchase the equipment and software, but also in the time required to input that information into the system. But a very important additional benefit is that we believe that the CAD system will also allow us to test alternative design ideas and that this testing may lead to even better quality of design.

MUSEUM-SPECIFIC ISSUES

It is this notion of visual quality that creates the issues specific to museum management. Recently, the Gallery obtained a gorgeous painting, The Martyrdom of Saint Bartholomew, by the Spanish painter Ribera. It was the first Ribera in our collection, and tremendously important to us not only for its singular beauty but also for its role in filling a gap in our collection. It was clear that there was a point beyond which the Gallery would not, and perhaps could not, go in paying for this beautiful work of art. Yet, to define how a curator or museum director makes such a judgment is almost impossible.

Similarly, we examine continuously the cost-effectiveness of our overall effort. We look at attendance to the permanent collection, and we look carefully at scholarly comment and at comment cards from individual members of our public. With exhibitions, we gauge attendance and watch reviews in the press and in scholarly journals. We also carefully manage the degree to which we spend our funds on these exhibitions through a series of exhibition budget meetings, post-mortem meetings at the end of each exhibition, and our own internal criticism of the results of our efforts. None of these variables makes sense in isolation, however, because we are concerned not only with the quantity of visitors, but also very much with the quality of the visit.

In our operating decisions, we face similar issues. We currently are discussing the question of the best hours to be open to the public. We have used some standard market research techniques to obtain visitors' views on the most desirable day of the week to be open late in the evening. Faced with our responsibility for taxpayers' money, we believe that it is most cost-effective to extend our hours on Friday evenings when more people can take advantage of the experience. Yet we have many devoted members of our public who were chagrined when the Gallery ceased its Sunday evening hours; they argued that it was the most beautiful time of the week to come see the pictures because they could see them in such quiet and solitude.

Another such quandary surfaces in weighing the cost-effectiveness of one research program against that of another. Research efforts can only be evaluated using fairly soft methods, such as the interest generated by the research among members of the scholarly community and the perception among serious and established scholars of the new scholarly contribution that would be made by such research program. The attendance at a seminar on one subject may be higher than at one on another subject, and we recognize that some topics can attract more private funding than others. Nevertheless, we resist using that measure to guide our choices, preferring to rely on complex judgments about scholarly quality and about the depth of new understanding produced by a given avenue of inquiry.

Among our security staff, the public service that they deliver is measured in many ways: through our comment cards from the public, the impact and impression they make on our donors, and, naturally, the avoidance of thefts and vandalism. In looking at security costs, it is clear, in one sense, that avoiding the loss of, or vandalism to, even one painting would more than justify almost any expenditure we could imagine making on security systems or staff. And yet, again, there is a limit to the money available. In this case, we look at reducing our risk to a level that we believe is acceptable. Only a soft judgment can be made as to what level of risk is acceptable, and this decision is similar to the one that the director has to make when he or she decides how much it is worth paying for a new acquisition for our collection.

With conservation, we face many such tricky issues. There is more work to be done than an army of conservators could undertake in a lifetime. And yet we have to trade off the growth of the staff and facilities and equipment for this endeavor against all the other needs of the Gallery. In this way, as in many others, the limits on what we are able to do are often the biggest help in deciding how much to do.

There are many such examples. We spend enormous energy on special events given to thank our corporate sponsors, our donors, and those who lend pictures to exhibitions. The long-term relationships and tangible financial gifts that come out of a given event are sometimes hard to measure. Nonetheless, the Gallery has seen over its history that the constant attention to the care and nurturing of these relationships has more than paid its way in the wonderful works of art and financial support given to the Gallery.

PROMOTING COST-EFFECTIVENESS

We have been asked the question, "What does the National Gallery do to promote cost-effectiveness?" I would cite first the fact that our budget process is very disciplined. Justifications must be given for every increase; some zero-based budgeting occurs from year to year, and this encourages people to examine alternative methods of getting the job done. There are competing demands for positions and for dollars, and each request engenders tough discussion about our priorities and how an addition of staff or budget will contribute to our mission. Second, what each department achieves with what it has to work with is measured against a perfectionist's standard for quality. Creativity and inventiveness are valued extremely highly, and, in this culture, making the most of what you have is extremely important. I also think that the Gallery trustees, in their choices of individuals for top management, encourage an attention to cost-effectiveness. Not only are they scholarly people, but also they are individuals with many years of management experience and advanced training in management.

If there is anything that the National Gallery of Art does to discourage attention to cost-effectiveness, it is that we take on too much at once. The bias for action and for speed that is so often a positive force sometimes drives us to solve a problem quickly and count the cost later.

In an institution that has such a bias for action, there are very few people dedicated to doing analysis. It is often necessary to make decisions using the information on hand, and, therefore, without a doubt our decisions are not always as cost effective as they might be. What I personally believe, however, after working in this environment for five years, is that it is healthier for an institution to have slightly too few resources for its aims and too few people to do analysis than to be in a situation in which every decision is analyzed to the "nth" degree and in which numerous staff are employed to do that job. There is a vitality that is created when an institution like the National Gallery continually sets out to accomplish more than any one of us thinks we can ever accomplish in the time available.

The Gallery is also relentlessly true to its mission. Let me give a final example of how the Gallery truly lives up to its belief in quality. In a recent exhibition the director, in reviewing the show the evening before it opened, commented that the objects in the last room might be more beautiful if the color of the walls were green instead of a rich brown. The staff worked overnight to change the color of the room and to re-silkscreen every label on the wall so that the best possible color could be on the walls for the next morning's opening.

This example illustrates how terribly important the statement "beauty is in the eye of the beholder" is in our business. Whether the step of repainting that gallery was cost effective is hard to answer. The manner in which it was done, through significant overtime expense, was the only means at our disposal. Because the new wall color was judged more beautiful, and because it could be done, it was done. The question asked was not "Should we do it?" The question was "Can we do it?"

NOTE

This chapter was adapted from remarks made by Anne Evans, Administrator, National Gallery of Art, at the June 1991 National Workshop on Cost-Effectiveness in the Nonprofit Sector, sponsored by TechnoServe and the School of Public Management of the Stanford University School of Business and funded by the Lilly Foundation.

3

Cost-Effectiveness in Youth Services: Preventing Adolescent Pregnancy

Heather Johnston Nicholson and
Faedra Lazar Weiss, *Girls, Inc.*

INTRODUCTION

Girls Incorporated, formerly Girls Clubs of America, is a national network of centers building girls' capacity for confident and competent adulthood in an inequitable world. This 46-year-old organization, through its affiliates and outreach programs in 122 cities, has a service population of over a quarter of a million, focusing on girls and young women from ages 6 through 18. While each Girls Incorporated affiliate schedules and implements programming independently, all share the mission and philosophy of Girls Incorporated and its focus on informal education through small-group, interactive programming for girls and young women. Girls Incorporated programming is developmental and comprehensive, involving six content categories, each with goals and objectives targeted to the special strengths and needs of girls. Affiliates are especially encouraged to make use of research-based programs addressing these areas, developed at the national level and by other affiliates.

PREVENTING ADOLESCENT PREGNANCY PROJECT

One of the areas in which Girls Incorporated affiliates are encouraged to provide programming is health and sexuality, enabling girls and young women to acquire information, practical and communications skills, and motivation to aid them in making responsible life choices. Out of these concerns grew the Preventing Adolescent Pregnancy project. This demonstration project included four components of a comprehensive program for girls aged 12 through 17. Girls aged 12 through 14 were eligible for Growing Together, a series of workshops designed to increase positive communication between parents (or other significant adults) and their daughters, and Will Power/Won't Power, an assertiveness training program with the specific goal of encouraging early adolescent girls to delay engaging in sexual intercourse. Older girls were eligible for Taking Care of Business, a structured program designed to increase adolescent girls' educational and career planning skills as well as their motivation and capacity to avoid pregnancy, and Health Bridge, a cooperative delivery system linking the educational opportunities available in Girls Incorporated centers with community-based health services, including reproductive health services.

Eight Girls Incorporated affiliates serving girls at high risk of adolescent pregnancy were selected for a longitudinal study of the Preventing Adolescent Pregnancy project's effectiveness. The project was implemented at four experimental (demonstration) sites; four control sites were to offer no new programming addressing the specific goals of the project to the target age groups for the three years of experimental program implementation. The program development and data collection phase of the Preventing Adolescent Pregnancy project ran from October 1985 through October 1988. In analyzing the data it became clear that the experimental and control sites were not well matched in background characteristics and risk of pregnancy. The analyses have thus been conducted using as a comparison group the young women from the four experimental sites who were eligible to participate in the programs and completed surveys, but who did not participate in the programs (see Nicholson & Postrado, 1992, for justification of this change in experimental design). Though there are some obvious drawbacks to this design, analyses of background characteristics indicate surprisingly little evidence of self-selection bias: The participants and the nonparticipants seem to be much alike in terms of characteristics associated with early pregnancy, including prior sexual experience. In effect, however, one of the major lessons of the Preventing Adolescent Pregnancy project is that the original eight-site design was not cost-effective. The four control sites made sacrifices for three years to produce data that will be subjected to only limited analysis.

Since the conclusion of the program development and data collection, Girls Incorporated has been analyzing the data produced by the project and implementing revised versions of the four components of the Preventing Adolescent Pregnancy program in Girls Incorporated centers nationwide.

Major support for Preventing Adolescent Pregnancy has been contributed by Carnegie Corporation of New York, William T. Grant Foundation, William and Flora Hewlett Foundation, Henry J. Kaiser Family Foundation, David and Lucile Packard Foundation, Prudential Foundation, and DeWitt Wallace-Reader's Digest Fund, Inc. Additional support has been contributed by foundations, corporations, and individuals at the national level and at participating sites.

Defining Cost-Effectiveness in Girls Incorporated

Girls Incorporated is committed to providing intentional, research-based programs that provide girls and young women with opportunities they are not getting in other settings.   With this in mind, several criteria emerge for determining what programming is cost-effective for Girls Incorporated:

• *Offer programs based on assessed community needs for girls.*   A program that uniquely meets a need in one community may be inappropriate in a second community, where the need has been adequately met by existing programs, may not even exist, or may be a relatively low priority compared to other needs of girls inadequately addressed locally.

• *Establish goals and objectives for programs, even if some are long-term goals not readily measured; evaluate outcomes unobtrusively.* Goals and objectives provide criteria by which to determine if a program does what it was designed to do.   A program designed to be educational that girls enjoy, but learn little from, is most likely not worth repeating without thoughtful revision.

• *Document costs of programs; compare costs with estimated outcomes for girls.*   A highly effective program that meets all of its goals and objectives, but reaches few girls, may be less cost-effective than a program that, while producing more modest results, can reach a larger number of girls. On the other hand, it is likely to be more expensive, but very important, to serve girls whose needs are not being well met by home, school, and community. Consider nonmonetary as well as monetary costs. Program implementation requires resources—staff time, space, slots on the Girls Incorporated center schedule—that once allocated to one program are not available for another.

• *Continue to offer programs that meet their objectives, meet high-priority needs of the girls and young women to whom they are offered, and have reasonable costs when conducted within the Girls Incorporated framework of small-group informal education.*

We have published more complete guidelines for affiliates to use in determining cost-effectiveness in *Assess for Success: Needs Assessment, Program Planning and Evaluation in Girls Incorporated* (Girls Incorporated, 1991).   We are presently adapting these guidelines for use by other youth-serving organizations.

Cost-Effectiveness in Preventing Adolescent Pregnancy

The Preventing Adolescent Pregnancy project lends itself to a study of cost-effectiveness for several reasons. First, cost-effectiveness is an obvious concern in a major impact study of a demonstration program expected to be replicated nationally. Similarly, cost-effectiveness is a large and increasingly sophisticated concern of major philanthropic organizations.   Most funders require accountability from grant recipients both during the course of a project, to see that it is being implemented as designed, and when the project has been completed, to assess the results of their investment. Demonstrated cost-effectiveness can be a key to continued support or to wider implementation.

By 1985, when the demonstration project was implemented, the costs to society of teen pregnancy were already at issue. Methods are available for calculating the monetary costs to society of teenage pregnancy and the cost savings for pregnancies delayed (Armstrong & Waszak, 1990; Burt & Haffner, 1986). No less important from the perspective of the young women at risk and of Girls Incorporated are the human costs to teenage women and their children. These concerns merit considerable investment of organizational resources. However, as pointed out above, Girls Incorporated affiliates must consider not only how effectively a program meets its goals and objectives, but also how much of their inevitably limited resources they would have to invest in that program, and therefore not in programs addressed to other, competing needs of girls, in order to implement it.

Similar questions of cost-effectiveness and expectations of accountability would arise in implementing a wide variety of programs. While specific costs and benefits will vary according to the issue addressed and the approach used, the methodology we used in calculating monetary costs and benefits of the Girls Incorporated Preventing Adolescent Pregnancy program can be adapted to other programs, as explained in the next section.

Methodology

The first step in determining the cost-effectiveness of the Preventing Adolescent Pregnancy project is calculating the number of pregnancies delayed.[1] Girls and young women aged 12 through 17 at the experimental sites completed surveys prior to the implementation of any programs and again annually for the three years of the program. They answered questions about their social and economic background, relationships with their parents, educational and career plans, and knowledge, attitudes, and behavior related to sexuality. The information they provided formed the data bases from which the overall rate of pregnancy among program participants and nonparticipants could be calculated.

Of particular interest were the rates of pregnancy among participants and nonparticipants in the total project and in the two program components designed for older adolescents, Taking Care of Business and Health Bridge. (Because of the young age of the participants in the other two project components designed for younger adolescents and the focus of these components on delaying the initiation of sexual intercourse, the additional impact of these components on pregnancy is likely to be measurable at a time beyond the duration of the demonstration project.) The number of pregnancies prevented (delayed) was

Table 3.1
Overall Estimate of Pregnancies Prevented (Delayed) in a Two-Year Period
by Participation in the Preventing Adolescent Pregnancy Project,
All Ages (12-20)

	Nonparticipant (n=147)	Participant (n=290)
no pregnancy	119 (81.0%)	257 (88.6%)
pregnancy	28 (19.0%)	33 (11.4%)

Difference in rate of pregnancy between nonparticipants and participants: 7.6 percent
$$.190 - .114 = .076$$

We therefore estimate that had the participants not participated in the Preventing Adolescent Pregnancy program, an additional 7.6 percent—22 young women—would have become pregnant during the time period of interest:
$$.076 \times 290 = 22.04$$

Source: Unpublished calculation, Leticia T. Postrado, Girls Incorporated National Resource Center, 1991.

estimated by calculating the rate of pregnancy among nonparticipants, subtracting the rate of pregnancy among participants and multiplying this differential rate by the number of participants (Table 3.1). For example, 28 of 147 young women between the ages of twelve and twenty who were nonparticipants (that is, they completed the annual surveys, but did not participate in the programs) reported becoming pregnant within a two-year period, as did 33 of 290 young women in the same age range who had participated in at least one program component during the two-year period as well as completing the annual surveys.   Thus, 19.0 percent of the nonparticipants, but only 11.4 percent of the participants became pregnant during this time, a difference of 7.6 percent. Assuming that the difference in rate was attributable to program participation, since the two groups were similar in all other respects, we estimated that had the 290 young women not participated in the Preventing Adolescent Pregnancy project, an additional 7.6 percent of them—22 young women—would probably have become pregnant during the period of interest. Similar calculations for the fourteen to twenty year-olds involved in the Taking Care of Business and Health Bridge program components and for those who served as controls for those participants estimate that these program components for older girls prevented (delayed) approximately four and five pregnancies, respectively (Tables 3.2 and 3.3). Note that this is

Table 3.2
Estimate of Pregnancies Prevented (Delayed) by Participation in the Taking Care of Business Program Component in a One-Year Period, Ages 14-20

	Nonparticipant 0 Hours (n=178)	Participated 1-12 Hours (n=64)	Participated 13-18 Hours (n=91)
no pregnancy	161 (90.4%)	56 (87.5%)	86 (94.5%)
pregnancy	17 (9.6%)	8 (12.5%)	5 (5.5%)

Difference in rate of pregnancy between nonparticipants and committed participants: 4.1 percent.

$$.096 - .055 = .041$$

Estimate of pregnancies prevented (delayed): 4

$$.041 \times 91 = 3.731$$

Source: Nicholson & Postrado (1991), Table 2.

Table 3.3
Estimate of Pregnancies Prevented (Delayed) by Participation in the Health Bridge Program Component in a One-Year Period, Ages 14-20

	Nonparticipant (n=265)	Participant (n=84)
no pregnancy	239 (90.2%)	81 (96.4%)
pregnancy	26 (9.8%)	3 (3.6%)

Difference in rate of pregnancy between nonparticipants and participants: 6.2 percent

$$.098 - .036 = .062[a]$$

Estimate of pregnancies prevented (delayed): 5

$$.062 \times 84 = 5.208$$

[a] Alternative formulation: $.062/.098 = .63$, estimating a 63 percent reduction in pregnancy rate.

Source: Nicholson & Postrado (1990), Table 2.

a conservative construction of the effect of the program components on pregnancy. The reduction from 19.0 to 11.4 percent is a 40 percent reduction in the rate of pregnancy and might have been used as the estimate of program effects.

Calculating the monetary costs of the Preventing Adolescent Pregnancy project seemed more straightforward than it has turned out to be. Demonstration sites were required to submit cost forms, identified as forms R, S and T, each year detailing expenses for implementing each program component. Many of these forms were in fact not submitted, and some of those that were did not break down costs as requested. In the project, priority was given both in follow-up and in designation, to forms tracking the participation of individual girls and young women. In a system of forms that began with A, it is perhaps not surprising that forms late in the alphabet received less attention.

The average cost per program component was calculated by combining costs for that component across years and across sites and dividing by the number of years and sites for which costs were reported. Similarly, by dividing the total reported cost of the program component by the number of participants served at those sites for the period reported, an average cost per participant was calculated for the Preventing Adolescent Pregnancy project as a whole and specifically for each program component.

These calculations are, of course, only as good as the data available. Only one of the four sites consistently submitted usable data. From the data we have, however, it is clear that staff training expenses, program start-up costs, and maximal or minimal registration for particular modules of a program component produced widely varying costs per year and per participant for a given project component. This is illustrated by the reported costs of implementing Growing Together (Table 3.4).

For these reasons, we calculated a second estimate of costs per program component based on the highest and lowest reported costs of implementation for three program components. For Health Bridge, we made our best estimate based on the little data we had. These estimates appear in Table 3.5.

Again, the program components had nonmonetary costs which must be considered in determining their cost-effectiveness. Some Girls Incorporated staff noticed that girls began to avoid them so as not to be approached to complete yet another survey or questionnaire. Staff at demonstration sites complained that the project as originally conceived, including three levels of each program component, would require so much staff time and room on the schedule that full implementation would virtually preclude offering any other programming for girls of the target ages. This did not happen because few girls chose to register for a second level of any program component. Still, there was some feeling that even partial implementation consumed too large a percentage of available resources, at the expense of programming for younger girls. Conversely, staff

Table 3.4
Estimate of Cost per Participant of Implementing the Growing Together Component of the Girls Incorporated Preventing Adolescent Pregnancy Program

	Cost per Year	Number of Participants	Average Cost
Affiliate 1, Year II	$ 5,590	16	$349
Affiliate 1, Year III	$ 7,868	14	$562
Affiliate 2, Year II	$ 8,187	20	$409
Total	$21,645	50	$433

at three of the four *control* sites experienced pressure from their boards and communities to address the serious issue of adolescent pregnancy. Guidelines had to be devised that allowed these affiliates to offer programming to girls too young for the Preventing Adolescent Pregnancy program, to take a leadership role in communitywide programming, and to refer girls of target age in urgent need of information or counseling to other agencies in order to serve the needs of Girls Incorporated members while maintaining the experimental design.

In 1989, the year in which the Preventing Adolescent Pregnancy project concluded, Armstrong and Waszak (1990, p. 7, Table II, figures for teenagers seventeen and under) estimated the potential savings to society of one teen pregnancy delayed until the mother was in her twenties as about $8,580, based on public investment in these families through Aid to Families with Dependent Children, Medicaid, and food stamps (Compare Armstrong & Waszak, 1990, pp. 4, 34-35 and Burt, 1986). This figure can be compared to the estimated cost per participant of implementing any given program component—$66 to $200 according to our best estimates. Figured this way, one could afford to offer a given program component to between 42 and 128 young women if one pregnancy were prevented (delayed) as a result. Similarly, multiplying $8,580 by the estimated number of pregnancies prevented by the Preventing Adolescent Pregnancy demonstration project provides a beginning estimate of the savings to society attributable to the implementation of the program, as shown in Table 3.6.

Figure 3.1 presents the complete algorithm for estimation of savings to society attributable to pregnancies delayed by participation in the Preventing Adolescent Pregnancy demonstration project.

Again, this methodology can be used to calculate costs of and savings from other programs that might be offered by nonprofit organizations. In a program with the desired outcome of avoiding drug and alcohol use, one could estimate the health care dollars that will not need to be spent on treating sequelae of sub-

Table 3.5
Estimate of Costs of Implementing Components of the Girls Incorporated
Preventing Adolescent Pregnancy Program

Program Component	Girls Served per Year	Cost per Year (high/low)* [average]	Cost per Girl served (high/low)*
Will Power/ Won't Power	75	$ 8,000/$ 5,000 [$ 6,500]	$106/$ 66 [$ 86]
Growing Together	40	$ 8,000/$ 5,000 [$ 6,500]	$200/$125 [$162]
Taking Care of Business	75	$ 8,000/$ 5,000 [$ 6,500]	$106/$ 66 [$ 86]
Health Bridge (one estimate)	50	$ 8,500	$170
Total [average]	240	$32,500/$23,500 [$28,000]	$136/$ 96 [$116]

At an average cost of $28,000 per year for implementing the entire Preventing Adolescent Pregnancy program, an affiliate could serve 240 girls for one year at an average cost of about $116 per girl.

* The estimated program costs of $5,000 to $8,000 per year, based on the reports of demonstration sites, include costs of program and administrative staff, local training, use of space at Girls Incorporated centers, basic supplies, local transportation and some educational resources. These figures assume that Preventing Adolescent Pregnancy is one of several programs offered by an existing, ongoing staff with an existing facility and an established membership base. These estimated costs do not include expenses for films and videotapes, which were provided free during the demonstration phase of the project.

stance abuse among the proportion of program participants who otherwise would have been expected to use these substances. For study of a diversionary program for first-time offenders, one could compare recidivism rates and calculate savings in the juvenile justice system. In evaluating a job training program, one might be able to collect comparative data not only on rate of employment, but also on wages; benefits could include estimates both of savings in welfare, Medicaid, and food stamps and of increased tax revenue collectible from people now gainfully employed. Figure 3.2 presents the algorithm comparing costs and savings adapted for general use.

Table 3.6
Estimate of Savings to Society Attributable to Pregnancies Prevented (Delayed) by Participation in the Preventing Adolescent Pregnancy Program

Program Component	Estimated Number of Pregnancies Delayed	Estimated Savings to Society Attributable to Program Participation	Estimated Cost of Program Component
any	22	$188,760	$33,640 ($116 x 290)
Taking Care of Business (committed participants)	4	$ 34,320	$ 7,826 ($86 x 91)
Health Bridge	5	$42,900	$14,280 ($170 x 84)

But not all costs of pregnancy or savings from pregnancy prevention or other programs are costs or savings to society, nor are they necessarily quantifiable. To some extent one can calculate and compare the costs of dropping out of school due to pregnancy or child care responsibilities versus the future earning power gained by completing high school, but the related issues of maturity and self-image are unquantifiable. It is similarly difficult to factor in the greater likelihood of the child of a teenage mother living below the poverty line or becoming a teenage parent in turn. On the positive side, we have no way of calculating what additional long-term benefits young women who chose to delay pregnancy gained. Some young women may have had the opportunity to choose from among a wider range of career options, perhaps by pursuing postsecondary education. Communication skills, particularly assertiveness, and contraceptive knowledge will continue to serve participants in establishing solid relationships and making sound decisions as to whether and when to bear children. Still, these unquantifiable costs and savings must be considered when determining whether the program components, individually and together, are cost-effective. Particularly in the case of pregnancy in early adolescence, it would be easy to justify an estimated cost two to three times the direct cost to society determined by Burt's criteria (1986, pp. 20-25 and *passim*; cf. Armstrong & Waszak, 1990, pp. 26-30 and Burt & Haffner, 1986, pp. 9, 11, 17).

Figure 3.1
Algorithm for Estimating the Savings to Society, Completed for the Preventing Adolescent Pregnancy Demonstration Project

Calculate:		Pregnancies prevented [from Table 3.1]

1.	19.0%	rate of pregnancy - nonparticipants
	- 11.4%	- rate of pregnancy - participants
	7.6%	difference in rate of pregnancy

2.	7.6%	difference in rate of pregnancy
	x 290.0	x total number of participants
	22.0	number of participants expected to have become pregnant without the program [rounded to nearest integer]

Calculate: Cost of program per participant [estimates from Table 3.5]

3. $ 116	average cost per participant
240/$28,000	number of participants/ cost per year

Estimate or Calculate: Savings to society for one pregnancy prevented (delayed)

4.	$8,580	[estimate based on Armstrong and Waszak, Table II]

Calculate: Savings to society attributable to program participation [cf. Table 3.6]

5.	22	number of pregnancies prevented [from 3.2, above]
	x $ 8,580	savings for one pregnancy prevented [from 3.4, above]
	$188,760	savings attributable to program participation

Calculate: Actual cost of program or estimated cost of program

6.	$116	average cost per participant [from 3.3, above]
	x 290	number of participants [from 3.2, above]
	$33,640	estimated cost of program [cf. Table 3.6]

Compare: savings (greater than, equal to, less than) cost of program
                         or   ratio of savings to cost of program

7.	$188,760	estimated savings [from 3.5, above] greater than
	$ 33,640	estimated cost of program [from 3.6, above]
	5.6:1	*estimated savings* = ratio of savings to cost of program
		estimated cost

Figure 3.2
Algorithm for Estimation of Savings to Society Attributable to an Intervention

Calculate:	Rate of desirable outcome*

1.
          rate of desirable outcome - participants
-     <u>rate of desirable outcome - nonparticipants</u>
          difference in rate of desirable outcome*

* If the outcome being measured is undesirable (e.g., drug use), the difference in rate should be a negative number if the intervention is successful. Use the absolute value of this number in subsequent calculations.

2.
          difference in rate of desirable outcome
x   <u>total number of participants</u>
          number of participants expected not to have experienced desirable outcome without intervention
          [rounded to nearest integer]

Calculate: Cost of intervention per participant

3.
          <u>average cost per participant</u>
          number of/cost per period of implementation participants

Estimate or Calculate: Savings to society for one participant achieving desirable outcome

4.

Calculate: Savings to society attributable to intervention

5.
          number of participants achieving desirable outcome
x   <u>society's savings per participant achieving desirable outcome</u>
          savings attributable to intervention

Calculate: Actual cost of intervention *or* estimated cost of intervention

6.
          average cost per participant
x   <u>number of participants</u>
          estimated cost of intervention

Compare: Savings attributable to intervention to cost of intervention *or* ratio of savings to cost of intervention

7.
          estimated/calculated savings [ideally, greater than] estimated/calculated cost of intervention

          <u>*estimated savings*</u> = ratio of savings to cost of program
          estimated cost

Figure 3.3
Form for Calculating Program Implementation Costs

Use the following form to calculate your program's total direct costs:

PROGRAM COSTS

Agency Name_____

Calculated for period from_____to _____

Calculated for program(s) _____

Completed by _____ Date _____

ITEM	COST
Staff time (including planning)	_____
Supplies	_____
Space	_____
Transportation	_____
Equipment	_____
Educational resources	_____
Promotional materials	_____
Office expenses	_____
Specialized training expenses	_____
Consultant fees	_____
Other: _____	_____

TOTAL PROGRAM COSTS   _____

NUMBER OF GIRLS SERVED   _____

TOTAL PROGRAM COSTS/NUMBER OF GIRLS SERVED = PROGRAM COST PER GIRL

Cost factors can provide a basis by which to compare and choose among effective programs. Also, many funders will require information on program costs as part of an evaluation or end-of-program report. Were the figures you recorded during the planning stage the actual costs?

When a program component is easy to deliver, using available staff and schedule time and other resources efficiently, even small positive results justify its cost-effectiveness (cf. Nicholson & Postrado, 1992). This turned out to be the case with Will Power/Won't Power, which utilized readily available audiovisual materials and skills that Girls Incorporated staff often already possessed and which was generally popular among the girls who took it—once. (They did balk at repeating advanced versions of the program, as called for in the project protocol.) On the other hand, Growing Together turned out to be quite costly to implement. Recruiting parents to participate along with their daughters proved quite difficult, and parents did not attend consistently, both of which resulted in a greater investment of staff time. Transportation, snacks, and care for younger siblings proved helpful in both regards, but constituted an additional expense. Staff also speculated that parents were reluctant to sign up for a program addressing issues related to sexuality with daughters who were already in dating relationships and in many cases seemed to be better informed than were their parents. One result of the demonstration project is that Growing Together, redesigned to take younger girls' lesser maturity into account, is now offered to nine- to eleven-year-olds and their parents.

Looking at the program components for older girls, Taking Care of Business was the program that was relatively easy and inexpensive to implement—in fact, many Girls Incorporated affiliates had been offering Choices, a version of this program more specifically focused on life and career planning, for some time. Still, it is difficult for any youth organization to attract and retain young women of this age, most of whom have school activities, jobs, or both competing for their time, and the effectiveness of Taking Care of Business in persuading teen women to delay pregnancy was strongly related to their commitment to the program component as measured by consistent attendance (cf. Nicholson & Postrado, 1991). Sites were most successful in implementing Taking Care of Business as part of a job training program.

The designers of Health Bridge had optimistically—but falsely—assumed that local clinics would donate staff time and services and underestimated the complexities boards of directors would see in the issues of confidentiality versus the need for parental consent in providing health services to minors and in providing transportation to allow participants to take advantage of health services. Thus, Health Bridge turned out to be burdensome to develop and expensive to implement. However, it was extremely well received, and also desperately needed in some communities, especially those in which the political climate does not allow for comprehensive clinics associated with schools.

The results of the demonstration project indicate that one or more program components are better than none. An affiliate might therefore begin with the components most easily and economically offered. This would certainly include Will Power/Won't Power and possibly also Taking Care of Business, if it provides services teenage women are not receiving elsewhere and if a recruitment base of teenage women who can be reasonably expected to display high commitment to the program is available at the Girls Incorporated center or in conjunction with other organizations. These programs might then stimulate interest in and funding for the more costly and less easily implemented components.

APPLYING COST-EFFECTIVENESS TECHNIQUES IN GIRLS INCORPORATED CENTERS

A revised version of the Preventing Adolescent Pregnancy project is now being implemented by Girls Incorporated affiliates throughout the United States, which are able to use national data from the Preventing Adolescent Pregnancy demonstration project to anticipate cost-effectiveness locally and to provide evidence of cost—effectiveness when applying for funding. The form by which affiliates can calculate program implementation costs has been modified and simplified, again based on experience in the demonstration project (Figure 3.3).

A study costing $2 million over six years is a very costly way to estimate three little figures: four pregnancies prevented by Taking Care of Business, five by Health Bridge, and twenty-two by the Preventing Adolescent Pregnancy program as a whole. Still, scientific evaluation is costly, and it is necessary to provide a sound basis for determining project effectiveness. It is especially difficult, time-consuming, and costly to determine the effectiveness of a project the major goal of which is prevention of an outcome. However, Girls Incorporated affiliates—and other nonprofit organizations—need accessible methods of determining which programs are most cost-effective and worth offering consistently, in the absence of a project on the scale of Preventing Adolescent Pregnancy, taking into account both the quantifiable and the unquantifiable outcomes of their programs. *Assess for Success* (Girls Incorporated, 1991) provides numerous suggestions for making such determinations:

- Many types of outcomes, falling under the general categories of knowledge, attitudes, and behavior, can be measured.

- A wide variety of techniques can be used to measure outcomes, ranging from attendance records and contracts to staff logs and expert observation and even pre- and post-tests.

- Measures of outcome may be objective (11.4 percent of the program participants, compared to 19.0 percent of the nonparticipants, became pregnant during the time period of interest), anecdotal (staff noted that more girls were asking for information about sex or sexuality and that most of these girls had participated in the program component), or somewhere in between (at the conclusion of the program component, 80 percent of the participants were able to give three reasons why becoming a teenage mother would interfere with their educational and career aspirations).

● In voluntary youth programs, written pre- and post-questionnaires and other paper-and-pencil intrusions often interfere with the liveliness and spontaneity of informal learning. Objectives built on observable behaviors and then observed are preferable.

COST-EFFECTIVENESS OF CONDUCTING COST-EFFECTIVENESS ANALYSIS

Was cost-effectiveness analysis of the Preventing Adolescent Pregnancy project cost-effective? To begin with, we do not have all the quantifiable data we would like since only one of the four experimental sites consistently provided the requested yearly reports of project expenditures. On the unquantifiable side, at both demonstration and control sites, the evaluation tail threatened to wag the program dog—in the former case by overloading staff and participants with required programming at the expense of other worthy programs and in the latter by preventing affiliates from offering programming beneficial to their members. Cost-effectiveness is as much a state of mind as a set of tools. The demonstration project consumed $2 million and a massive amount of Girls Incorporated staff and membership time, patience, and goodwill.

More positively, the Preventing Adolescent Pregnancy project is one of the few projects of this scope. Our estimate that participation prevented (delayed) approximately twenty-two pregnancies implies a savings to society minimally approaching $200,000 and potentially several times that great. The project also produced unquantifiable benefits. The scale of the study not only allowed us to estimate the number of pregnancies prevented (delayed), but also provided a large enough data base to permit consideration of some effects of participation, controlling for such variables as mother's education, academic performance, and level of participation. (Even so, the study was not large enough to allow for analysis controlling for every variable of potential interest.) The demonstration project also afforded the opportunity to refine the program components so that they can be offered as effectively and inexpensively as possible to a large number of girls and young women. Its reasonably sophisticated research design provided a great deal of support for the affiliates, which do not have the resources for such a massive evaluation, but which need to know, when making their own programming decisions and when seeking funding, that these programs do work. In addition, many other organizations and individuals are interested in preventing adolescent pregnancy. Through their participation in the Preventing Adolescent Pregnancy project, affiliates serving as both experimental and control sites gained recognition in their communities as experts on this important issue. On the national level, Girls Incorporated—through a highly visible release of the important findings, several forthcoming articles, and networking—is sharing new information about preventing adolescent pregnancy.

Lessons Learned

Here are some of the things we learned from the Preventing Adolescent Pregnancy project:

- Design research, including cost-effectiveness analysis, that does not unduly burden the staff or participants. In this project, enthusiasm remained remarkably high despite unreasonable demands.

- Follow up early and often. Earlier attention to the fact that many cost reports were not being turned in might have led us to work with the experimental affiliates to provide these important data in another form. And, if possible, limit the number of forms to be completed—avoid attempts to collect all possible data in a single study. Similarly, rapid preliminary analysis of the first year's worth of annual surveys might have led to realization at that point that the control sites were in fact not appropriate controls for the experimental sites.

- Plan for the confidence you need to have in your estimates of cost-effectiveness. Methods of evaluation range from the simple and inexpensive, though not scientifically rigorous, to the very expensive, but more clearly supportable. The method you choose will depend on the audience for your cost-effectiveness analysis.

- Consider the ratio of program cost to number of participants. In other words, rather than jumping into an expensive program and serving only a few participants, invest in marketing strategies to ensure sufficient registration and retention.

- Work with staff and youth to develop systems of cost-effectiveness that meet their needs. Use the concepts often to develop habits of thinking about whether programs are worth the effort to all involved.

NOTES

The authors wish to acknowledge the significant contributions of Jane Quinn, currently with the Carnegie Council on Adolescent Development, Catherine H. Smith, Julie K. Hamm, and Ellen Wahl of the Girls Incorporated national staff; curriculum developer and advisor Pamela M. Wilson; and other members of the advisory panel for the Preventing Adolescent pregnancy Project, Joy G. Dryfoos, Frank F. Furstenberg, Jr., Irma R. Hilton, and Douglas Kirby. Special thanks are also due the staff, board, and members of the eight Girls Incorporated affiliates that made the project possible. The authors are solely responsible for the findings and interpretations.

1. While the project title was—appropriately—Preventing Adolescent Pregnancy, preventing pregnancy during adolescence is tantamount to delaying pregnancy among participants. Most participants will eventually become mothers, but ideally at a later age

than they otherwise might have.

REFERENCES

Armstrong, E., and C. Waszak. *Teenage Pregnancy and Too-Early Childbearing: Public Costs, Personal Consequences*. Washington, D.C.: Center for Population Options, 1990.

Burt, M. *Estimates of Public Costs for Teenage Childbearing: A Review of Recent Studies and Estimates of 1985 Public Costs*. Washington, D.C.: Center for Population Options, 1986.

Burt, M., and D. Haffner. *Teenage Childbearing: How Much Does It Cost?* Washington, D.C.: Center for Population Options, 1986.

Girls Incorporated. *Assess for Success: Needs Assessment, Program Planning and Evaluation in Girls Incorporated*. Indianapolis: Author, 1991.

Nicholson, H. J., and L. T. Postrado. "HEALTH BRIDGE™: A Collaborative Model for Delivering Health Services to Young Women Ages 12-18." Paper presented at the National Organization on Pregnancy and Parenting, Inc., Annual Conference, 1990. October 18-20, Atlanta.

Nicholson, H. J., and L. T. Postrado. "Effectiveness of Taking Care of Business: A Life Options Component of the Girls Incorporated Preventing Adolescent Pregnancy Program." Submitted for publication, 1991.

Nicholson, H. J., and L. T. Postrado. "A Comprehensive Age-Phased Approach: Girls Incorporated." In *Preventing Adolescent Pregnancy: Model Programs and Evaluations*, edited by B. C. Miller, J. J. Card, R. Paikoff, and J. L. Peterson. Newbury Park, Calif.: Sage Publications, 1992.

4

Foundations of Cost-Effectiveness Analysis for Health and Medical Practices

Milton C. Weinstein and William B. Stason

It is now almost universally believed that the resources available to meet the demands for health care are limited. This fact was not, perhaps, perceived a few decades ago, before health insurance became so pervasive and before medical technologies had proliferated to the extent that they have today. In 1976, with the United States spending over $120 Billion a year on health care and with this expenditure increasing at a rate nearly double that of the gross national product, it is a virtual certainty that limits will somehow be set. We, as a nation, will have to think very carefully about how to allocate the resources we are willing to make available for health care (Hiatt, 1975).

Already, decisions are being made. Hospitals that must ration beds, physicians who must allocate their time, and fiscal intermediaries that must establish reimbursement policies are all implicitly setting priorities for the use of health resources. The availability of health care facilities and providers also sets limits and forces difficult decisions. Such decisions, however, are often inconsistent, not only with each other, but also with the societal objective of deriving the maximum health benefits from the dollars spent. For example, one widely practiced medical procedure may be costing many thousands or even hundreds of thousands of dollars per year of life saved (or per year of limited activity or discomfort prevented), whereas another procedure that is restricted in use could be expected to save several times as many years of life (or years of good health) for the same expenditure. To facilitate these critical allocation decisions, the best current information on both the efficacy of medical practices and their costs must be made available to decision makers in a systematic fashion that will allow them to make valid comparisons among alternative uses of resources. To implement the conclusions from such comparisons, incentives must be offered to providers and patients alike to adopt cost-effective health practices.

In this context, increasingly frequent studies have sought to guide present and future decisions by systematic analysis (Weinstein & Stason, 1976; Bunker, Mosteller & Barnes, 1977). These efforts, based on such approaches as benefit-cost analysis, cost-effectiveness analysis and decision analysis, attempt to use existing information in a given area of health care to develop criteria for allocating resources.   Such approaches have potential value for allocation decisions both within a categorical health problem and across diseases or health problems. If these approaches were to become widely understood and accepted by the key decision makers in the health care sector, including the physician, important health benefits or cost savings might be realized. The purpose of this chapter is to describe the basic foundations of the methods of cost-effectiveness analysis used in the allocation of health care resources.

PREREQUISITES FOR USEFUL COST-EFFECTIVENESS ANALYSIS

Many analyses have not been accepted by health care decision makers because a critical factor or issue has been omitted. The reason is that, in the attempt to be "objective," the analyst may avoid uncertainties or intangibles that often dominate the decision maker's thought process.   A useful cost-effectiveness analysis must be comprehensive and broadly applicable.

Although it is useful to take the overall societal point of view in evaluating alternative allocations of health resources (i.e., by measuring aggregate cost and aggregate health benefits across all members of society), it is also important to consider the particular objectives of the actual decision makers. For example, total costs might be of concern to a health maintenance organization, whereas only non reimbursable costs might be of concern to a group practice affiliated with a separate fiscal intermediary. Society as a whole bears all the costs, whether through insurance premiums or out-of-pocket payments, but the organizations and individuals who actually make resource-allocation decisions usually have varying objectives that should be recognized in a realistic cost-effectiveness analysis.

The estimates of medical effectiveness and cost that enter into an analysis should be expressed to reflect explicitly the uncertainties surrounding those estimates.   The available data base on the effectiveness of most clinical procedures is distressingly limited. Nevertheless, the tendency among health professionals to demand objective, scientifically valid proof, though laudable, begs the necessity to use the best available evidence, however uncertain, to make today's resource-allocation decisions.   A responsible analysis should be structured to incorporate new information as it becomes available and should be used to suggest areas requiring future research to resolve critical uncertainties.

The measures of effectiveness of health practices used in the analysis should be outcome oriented, with length of life and quality of life as the ultimate measures. Process measures are often useful as proxies for outcome measures when the latter are not available, but an analysis that stops at that point is less useful in guiding resource allocation. To be explicit about quality of life, and possible trade-offs between longevity and quality, subjective values are necessarily involved. A useful analysis should serve the important function of incorporating these values into a rational framework for decision making.

Finally, the trade-offs between present and future health benefits and costs must be considered. This consideration is particularly important for screening or preventive programs for which the costs are immediate, but the health benefits are in the future. The appropriate use of discounting procedures is essential to adjust for these temporal discrepancies.

GENERAL ANALYTIC APPROACHES

Cost-effectiveness analysis and benefit-cost (or cost-benefit) analysis are two related, but quite different, approaches to the assessment of health practices. Confusion frequently exists between the two approaches: Many analyses that are technically cost-effectiveness analyses are often labeled "cost-benefit" analyses, and vice versa. The key distinction is that a benefit-cost analysis must value all outcomes in economic (e.g., dollar) terms, including lives or years of life and morbidity, whereas a cost-effectiveness analysis serves to place priorities on alternative expenditures without requiring that the dollar values of life and health be assessed.

The underlying premise of cost-effectiveness analysis in health problems (Weinstein & Stason, 1976; Acton, 1973; Zeckhauser, 1975) is that, for any given level of resources available, society (or the decision-making jurisdiction involved) wishes to maximize the total aggregate health benefits conferred. Alternatively, for a given health benefit goal, the objective is to minimize the cost of achieving it. In either formulation, the analytical methodology is the same. First of all, health benefits and health-resource costs must each be expressed in terms of some common unit of measurement. Health-resource costs are inevitably measured in dollars. Health benefits, or health-effectiveness, may be expressed in a variety of ways, the most common being either lives or life years, or some variant of them. The use of quality-adjusted life years has the advantage of incorporating changes in survival and morbidity in a single measure that reflects trade-offs between them. The ratio of costs to benefits, expressed as cost per year of life saved or cost per quality-adjusted year of life saved, becomes the cost-effectiveness measure. Alternative programs or services are then ranked, from the lowest value of this cost-per-unit-effectiveness ratio to the highest, and selected from the top until available resources are exhausted. The point on the priority list at which the available resources are exhausted, or at which society is no longer willing to pay the price for the benefits achieved, becomes society's cutoff level of permissible cost-per-unit-effectiveness. For example, the level of blood pressure at which antihypertensive treatment is recommended might be based on the corresponding cost-effectiveness cutoff level. (See Stason & Weinstein, 1977, for examples of this and other concepts presented in this chapter.) Application of this procedure ensures that the maximum possible expected health benefit is realized, subject to whatever resource constraint is in effect.

Benefit-cost analysis (Klarman, 1973; Weisbrod, 1961) has been applied in many health contexts, ranging from mobile coronary care units to venereal disease control programs (Klarman, 1965). To value life years and quality of life in dollars, the traditional approach is to use the annual earnings of a worker as a measure of the value of a productive year of life (Rice, 1967; Weisbrod, 1961). The value of time lost from work is similarly calculated. The rationale is that society, including the individual in question, would lose potential consumption of goods and services in proportion to lost productivity. Critics of the lost-earnings approach have argued that it fails to take into account many subjective values associated with health and life that are not captured by earnings alone. Some favor, as alternatives, the assessment of individual willingness to pay to reduce the probabilities of death and disease (Acton, 1973, 1975; Schelling, 1968) or the imputation of the added wages that workers in hazardous jobs require as compensation for their risks (Thaler & Rosen, 1976). Once benefits and costs have been somehow expressed in dollar terms, net benefits are derived as the difference between the two: If the results are positive, the argument goes, the program or practice should be undertaken and If negative, it should not.

The major disadvantage of the benefit-cost framework is that human lives and quality of life must be valued in dollars. Many decision makers find this point difficult and do not trust analyses that depend on such valuations. Cost-effectiveness analysis, on the other hand, requires only that health outcomes be expressed in commensurate units (e.g., quality-adjusted life years), generally involving trade-offs more palatable to physicians. An advantage of the benefit-cost framework is that it leads to a positive or negative (or zero) number for each program or practice evaluated and, therefore, does not require knowledge of a cost-effectiveness cutoff level to decide whether a particular practice should be undertaken. Finally, a limitation of both approaches is that the benefits and costs to individual members of society need to be aggregated. If the equitable distribution benefits and costs across individuals or groups are of concern, a single cost-effectiveness measure will not do. However, as economists are wont to argue, over large numbers of programs and practices the inequities are likely to even themselves out and, with some exceptions, may reasonably be ignored.

The technics of decision analysis (Raffa, 1968; Schwartz et al., 1973; Schoenbaum, McNeill & Kavet, 1976; Parker 1976) are, in our opinion, essential adjuncts to either cost-effectiveness or benefit-cost analysis. Decision analysis provides a cohesive framework for dealing with both uncertainty and complex value judgments, as well as with the complex sequencing of decisions based on the current level of information. Since all these elements are usually present, the ensuing description of the elements of cost-effectiveness analysis includes many technics drawn from this field.

ELEMENTS OF COST-EFFECTIVENESS ANALYSIS

Cost-Effectiveness Ratio

The criterion for cost-effectiveness is the ratio of the net increase of health care costs to the net effectiveness in terms of enhanced life expectancy and quality of life. The lower the value of this ratio, the higher the priority in terms of maximizing benefits derived from a given health expenditure.

The rationale for the division between the elements of the numerator (cost) and the denominator (effectiveness) is straightforward. The former includes only resources drawn from the health care budget; it describes the net change in the total number of dollars spent on health care as a result of the program or practice in question. The denominator, net health-effectiveness, includes the life and other health benefits conferred, measured in lives, life years, or quality-adjusted life years.

Net Health Care Costs

Analytically, the net health care costs (ΔC) of a program or practice may be calculated from the following expression:

$$\Delta C = \Delta C_{Rx} + \Delta C_{SE} - \Delta C_{Morb} + \Delta CRx\Delta LE \qquad (1)$$

The first component (ΔC_{Rx}) includes all direct medical and health care costs. It includes the costs of hospitalization, physician time, medications, laboratory services, counseling, and other ancillary services. The second component (ΔC_{SE}) includes all health care costs associated with the adverse side effects of treatment. The third component (ΔC_{Morb}) enters with a minus sign because it refers to savings in health care, rehabilitation and custodial costs due to the prevention or alleviation of disease. The final component ($\Delta C_{Rx\Delta LE}$) includes the costs of treating diseases that would not have occurred if the patient had not lived longer as a result of the original treatment. Thus, a patient whose antihypertensive treatment is associated with the prevention of death from an early stroke, but who later in life requires treatment for a malignant neoplasm, would incur costs in this category.

This definition of net medical care costs, requires some explanation. In the first place, decision makers who do not adopt the societal perspective may not wish to include components of cost that they do not bear out-of-pocket. Third-party payers who reimburse hospital costs but not medications, may exclude the latter from their definition of cost. Individual physicians or group practices may not be constrained at all by cost as defined here, but rather by their available time and by the resources available to their patients in paying any required out-of-pocket costs. Health maintenance organizations, however, may come closest to bearing internally all the health care costs that society at large must bear. Second, our definition of net health care costs does not include lost earnings due to time missed from work, despite the fact that the loss of productivity may have financial consequences for individuals and society. Instead, it is more consistent with the rationale for the cost-effectiveness ratio to combine all health benefits, including those associated with reduced morbidity and disability, in the measure of net health-effectiveness, while including in the dollar costs only the components that add to or subtract from the resources available for health care.

Net Health-Effectiveness

The basic quantitative measure of health-effectiveness is the increase in expected number of life years. Given a schedule of age-specific mortality probabilities with and without the program or practice in question, it is a straightforward matter of life-table analysis to compute life expectancies with and without the program or practice, the difference being the expected net increase in life years (ΔY).

It has become more and more evident, however, that the effects of health practices on the quality of life occupy an equally prominent role in the objectives of providers and consumers of health care. On the one hand, concern over the often highly subjective side effects of medications must somehow be factored into the analysis. On the other hand, the quality-of-life-improving effects of an operation are frequently more important considerations than is its effect on longevity (Bunker, 1974). A year of life for a patient on renal hemodialysis or for one who has chronic disability from a severe cerebrovascular accident must surely be counted differently than is a completely healthy year.

Although still controversial, methods for explicitly incorporating quality-of-life concerns into formal cost-effectiveness analyses are becoming more widely used and accepted (Weinstein & Stason, 1976; Torrency, Sackett & Thomas, 1973; Bush, Chen & Patrick, 1973; Pliskin & Beck, 1976). The general approach that has been used is to derive some measure like quality-adjusted life years to express the total health effect in common units. The first approaches to this problem fall under the rubric of health status indexes (Torrency, Sackett & Thomas, 1973; Bush, Chen & Patrick, 1973). A health status index is essentially a weighting scheme: Each definable health status—ranging from death to coma to varying degrees of disability and discomfort to full health, and accounting for age differences—is assigned a weight from zero to one, and the number of years spent at a given health status, Y_s, is multiplied by the corresponding weight, λ_S, to yield a number, $\lambda_S Y_S$, that might be thought of as an equivalent number of years with full health—a number of quality-adjusted life years (QALYs). The source of these weights is ultimately subjective and can be thought of as reflecting answers to either of the following questions: "Taking into account your age, pain and suffering, immobility, and lost earnings, what fraction, P, of a year of life would you be willing to give up to be completely healthy for the remaining fraction of a year instead of maintaining your present level of health status for the full year?" Or "Taking into account these same factors, what probability, P, of death would you be willing to accept so that, if you survived, you would have full health rather than your present health status for the rest of your life?" In both cases, an answer of P near 1.0 would imply that the health status is nearly as bad as death; an answer near 0.0 would imply a mild or negligible level of disability. The weight, λ_S, above would correspond to 1 - P.

Clearly, different people would answer these questions differently. In a cost-effectiveness analysis at the societal level, it is therefore essential that a range of possible weights be used to reflect the spectrum of individual values.

The expected number of quality-adjusted life years is then the expected number of unadjusted life years (ΔY), adjusted for improvements in the quality-of-life years due to the alleviation or prevention of morbidity (ΔY_{Morb}) and for side effects of treatment (ΔY_{SE}). The sum

$$\Delta E = \Delta Y + \Delta Y_{Morb} - \Delta YSE \qquad (2)$$

thus represents the net health-effectiveness of the program or practice in question, measured in QALYs.

This trade-off concept is difficult. Most analyses avoid quality-of-life considerations entirely, quantifying only the change in life expectancy. Where the quality-of-life effects are believed to be important, however, the credibility of an otherwise effective analysis may be jeopardized. Trade-offs involving quality-of-life considerations are made implicitly by health care decision makers all the time; the role of the analysis is to make them explicit.

Discounting Future Costs and Health Benefits: Present-Value Analysis

Rarely do all costs and benefits occur at the same time. It is therefore necessary to combine present and future costs, as well as present and future benefits, in comparable units. One simple way would be to add up all dollar costs, regardless of when they are incurred, and all benefits, regardless of when they occur. This procedure, however, ignores the fact that a dollar in 1977 is worth more than it will be in 1978 or 2077. Present-value analysis is a widely accepted method of weighting future dollars by a discount factor to make them comparable to present dollars. For consistency, the same discount factor should be applied to future health benefits (i.e., quality-adjusted life years) as well.

On the dollar-cost side, two factors cause us to weight future costs less heavily. One is inflation: A dollar in 1977 can purchase more goods and services than a dollar will in 1978. By inflation, the dollar is essentially revalued. What is often misunderstood, however, is that inflation is not the reason for discounting future costs.

Even if all costs, present and future, are expressed as *real current dollars* (i.e., dollars adjusted for the rate of inflation), future costs still need to be discounted. The reason is that a dollar not spent now can be invested productively to yield a larger number of real dollars in the future. Assuming an annual return of 5 percent, it follows that $X spent n years hence should be valued in present terms as $X/(1.05)^n$ because this quantity invested at 5 percent would yield $X in n years. This is the present-value of $X spent n years in the future at a discount rate of 5 percent. The cost terms in the numerator of the cost-effectiveness ratio are computed, then, as present-value costs, the selected discount rate being used.

Although it is unquestioned among economists that dollar costs should be discounted, far more controversial is the rate at which they should be discounted. In large part, differences of opinion stem from the variations among interest rates observed in our economy, which, in turn, reflect differences between the productive potential of investment in capital and individual preferences for present versus future consumption of goods and services. Currently, economists espouse discount rates, after correcting for inflation, as high as 10 percent (the rate used by the U.S. Office of Management and Budget, subject to much criticism) or as low as 0 (or negative) percent; consensus generally lies between 4 and 6 percent. In any cost-effectiveness or benefit-cost analysis, a range of discount rates should be tested.

On the health benefit side, the use of discounting requires more justification. For programs involving screening for disease, where the life years saved are far in the future, it matters a great deal whether expected benefits are discounted. Without discounting, a program that saves one QALY forty years hence at a present-value cost of $10,000 would have a cost-effectiveness ratio of $10,000 per QALY. With discounting at 5 percent per year, the present value of that future QALY is reduced to $1/(1.05)^{40}$ or about 0.14, and the ratio becomes $70,000 per QALY, a remarkable difference in the implied priority of the program in the range of possible alternative uses of health resources.

The reason for discounting future life years saved is not that life years can, in any sense, be invested to yield more life years as dollars can be invested to yield more dollars. Nor is it necessary to assume that life years in the future are less valuable than life years today in any absolute utilitarian sense. Rather, the reason for discounting future life years is precisely that they are being valued relative to dollars, and since a dollar in the future is discounted relative to a present dollar, so must a life year in the future be discounted relative to a present dollar. Consider the following example that illustrates the chain of logic for discounting future health benefits (Table 4.1). Suppose that Program A saves one year of life expectancy forty years hence at a present cost of $10,000 and that Program B saves one year of life expectancy now at a present cost of $10,000. Which program should have higher priority? To answer this question, consider first a hypothetical Program A_1, which can save one year of life forty years hence at a cost of $70,000 borne in forty years. This result is equivalent to Program A because $70,000 in forty ears has a present value (at 5 percent) of $10,000 and because the benefits of both Program A and Program A_1 are the same. Now, consider Program A_2, which simply translates both the benefits and the costs of Program A_1 from the future to the present. Provided life years are valued the same in relation to dollars in the present as in the future, Program A_2 should be considered to have the same long-run priority as Program A_1. Finally, consider Program A_3, under which both the benefits and the costs are reduced proportionately in relation to Program A_2 and which therefore has the same priority. Now, it is clear that Program B is preferable to Program A_3 since the costs are identical, but the benefits of Program B, which accrue at the same point in time as those of A_3, are much more. Moreover, we have seen that Program A_3, which has the same priority as Program A, could have been derived from Program A simply by discounting the future health benefits. The cost-effectiveness ratio for Program A is thus the present value of cost divided by the present value of benefit, or $10,000 \div [1/(1.05)^{40}]$, or $70,000 per QALY, which compares unfavorably to the $10,000 per QALY ratio for Program B.

Throughout this argument, it is never stated that, in any absolute sense, a year of life in the future is less valuable than a year of life in the present. It is the discounting of dollar costs, and the assumed constant steady-state relationship between dollars and health benefits, that mandates the discounting of health benefits (i.e., QALYs) as well as dollar health costs.

The exact equivalence between A_1 and A_2 that underlies this line of reasoning assumes that opportunities for purchasing health benefits for dollars do not change over time. If it is expected that technology will improve so that it becomes less expensive to save lives, A_2 may be somewhat less valuable than A_1, suggesting an even higher effective discount rate for life years than for dollar costs. If it is expected that environmental or other factors will conspire to make lifesaving more expensive—that is, more valuable—in the future, a lower discount rate may be in order. Moreover, if it is anticipated that societal attitudes will change so that the willingness to pay for lifesaving increases with time, a lower discount rate may be appropriate.

Another important caveat is that as we move far into the future, the uncertainty about the rate of discount that will obtain at that time increases, as

Table 4.1
Hypothetical Programs with Varying Timing of Costs and Health Benefits

PROGRAM	COST	BENEFIT
A	$10,000 now	1 yr of life expectancy in 40 yr
A_1	$70,000* in 40 yr	1 yr of life expectancy in 40 yr
A_2	$70,000 now	1 yr of life expectancy now
A_3	$10,000 now	$1/7 - 1/(1.05)^{40}$ yr of life expectancy now
B	$10,000 now	1 yr of life expectancy now

* $70,000 - $10,000 X 1.05^{40}

does the uncertainty concerning future uses of health resources that will be available. Hence, the discount rate should be varied over a range of possibilities if the benefits or costs occur in the distant future.

Sensitivity Analysis

Unfortunately, estimates of the benefits of health practices, in terms of mortality and morbidity probabilities, are rarely known with certainty. Often, there is some evidence of the degree of efficacy, but rarely are there quantitative measures sufficient to calculate with confidence differences in life expectancy, let alone differences in quality-adjusted life expectancy. The critics of cost-effectiveness analysis of health and medical practices argue that this uncertainty renders useless any attempts to quantify the benefits of such practices. Supporters argue, in retort, that decisions about resource allocation have to be made, and, although fully supporting efforts to improve the information base upon which to make decisions, they urge that the best available evidence, together with a range of subjective estimates where needed, be used in a coherent analytical framework to guide those decisions.

The most easily applied method available to deal with uncertainty   is sensitivity analysis. In this method, the most uncertain features and assumptions in the cost-effectiveness calculation are varied one at a time over the range of possible values. If the basic conclusions do not change when a particular feature or assumption is varied, confidence in the conclusion is increased. If, instead, the basic conclusions are sensitive to variations in a particular feature or assumption, further research to learn more about that feature may be especially valuable. Moreover, to make current decisions in the face of that uncertainty, more detailed decision analysis may be needed (Raffa, 1968; Schwartz et al., 1973).

Examples of sensitivity analyses that are often useful include varying the estimates of the degree of clinical efficacy of the procedure in question, varying the weights assigned to various quality levels in computing quality-adjusted life expectancy, and testing a range of discount rates, say, from 0 to 10 percent per year. Rather than avoiding such factors, which decimates the realism of the analysis, they should be included, but with ample sensitivity analysis to accommodate a wide range of beliefs and preferences.

CONCLUSIONS ON THE VALUE AND APPLICATION OF COST-EFFECTIVENESS ANALYSIS IN HEALTH CARE

The principal value of formal cost-effectiveness analysis in health care is that it forces one to be explicit about the beliefs and values that underlie allocation decisions. Opposing points of view can be clarified in terms of specific disagreements over assumptions, probability estimates, or value trade-offs.

Cost-effectiveness analysis often takes the societal point of view and is therefore directed at decision makers who act as agents for society as a whole. Nevertheless, the basic analytic framework should be useful to a variety of decision makers, who may include in the definitions of cost and benefit whatever elements they perceive to be within their domain. Such concepts as quality-adjusted life years, discounting, and sensitivity analysis are equally applicable to analyses directed at physicians, hospitals, and insurance programs. Moreover, as we as a nation move toward the creation of institutions that take on more of the societal perspective (e.g., national health insurance, health systems agencies, and health maintenance organizations), the importance and value of cost-effectiveness analysis will increase even more.

To facilitate such analyses, better data on the efficacy and costs of health practices are urgently needed. Application of the resource-allocation perspective, even with currently available data, can point to the kinds of data needed and the form in which the data should be collected. The design of clinical trials and observational studies should take this perspective into account.

The conclusions of an analysis that rests on uncertain data and subjective values, even with all possible sensitivity analysis, are bound to be interpreted as too definitive by some. Despite warnings that the conclusions must be updated as new evidence becomes available, users of an analysis may apply its conclusions to initiate programs that then build up their own momentum and are difficult to alter. Flexibility for change must be maintained. Nevertheless, resource-allocation decisions do have to be made, and the choice is often between relying upon a responsible analysis, with all its imperfections, and no analysis at all. The former, in these times of increasingly complex decisions, difficult trade-offs, and limited resources, is by far the preferred choice.

NOTE

This chapter is adapted from information appearing in *NEJM,* specifically from an article by Milton C. Weinstein and William B. Stason entitled "Foundations of Cost-Effectiveness Analysis for Health and Medical Practices," *New England Journal of Medicine* 296 (1977):716-721.

REFERENCES

Acton, J. P. *Evaluating Public Programs to Save Lives: The Case of Heart Attacks* Rand Corporation Report R-950-RC. Santa Monica, Calif.: Rand Corp, 1973.

Acton, J. P. *Measuring the Social Impact of Heart and Circulatory Disease Programs: Preliminary Framework and Estimates.* Rand Corporation Report R-1697-NHLI. Santa Monica, Calif.: Rand Corp., 1975.

Bunker, J. "Risks and Benefits of Surgery." In *Benefits and Risks in Medical Care: A Symposium Held by the Office of Health Economics,* edited by D. Taylor, 85-91. Luton, England: White Crescent Press, 1974.

Bunker, J. P., C. F. Mosteller, and B. A. Barnes. *Costs, Risks and Benefits of Surgery.* New York: Oxford University Press, 1977.

Bush, J. W., M. M. Chen, and D. L. Patrick. "Health Status Index in Cost-Effectiveness Analysis of PKU Program." In *Health Status Indexes: Proceedings of a Conference Conducted by Health Services Research,* edited by R. L. Berg. Chicago: Hospital Research and Educational Trust, 1973.

Hiatt, H. H. "Protecting the Medical Commons: Who Is Responsible?" *New England Journal of Medicine* 293 (1975): 235-41.

Klarman, H.E. "Syphilis Control Programs." In *Measuring Benefits of Government Investments,* edited by R. Dorfman, 367-414.   Washington, D.C.: Brookings Institution, 1965.

Klarman, H.E. "Application of Cost-Benefit Systems Technology." In *Technology and Health Care Systems in the 1980's,* edited by M. F. Collen. (DHEW Publication No. [HSM]73-3016). Washington, D.C.: Government Printing Office, 1973.

McNeil, B. J., P. D. Varady, B. A. Burrows, and S.J. Adelstein. "Measures of Clinical Efficacy: Cost-Effectiveness Calculations in the Diagnosis and Treatment of Hypertensive Renovascular Disease." *New England Journal of Medicine* 293 (1975): 216-221.

Neuhauser, D., and A. M. Lewicki. "What Do We Gain from the Sixth Stool Guaiac?" *New England Journal of Medicine* 293 (1975): 226-28.

Pauker, S. G. "Coronary Artery Surgery: the Use of Decision Analysis." *Annals of Internal Medicine* 85 (1976): 8-18.

Pliskin, J. S., and C. H. Beck, Jr. "A Health Index for Patient Selection: A Value Function Approach—With Application to Chronic Renal Failure Patients." *Management Science* 22 (1976): 1009-1021.

Raffa, H. *Decision Analysis: Introductory Lectures on Choices under Uncertainty.* Reading, Mass.: Addison-Wesley, 1968.

Rice, D. P. "Estimating the Cost of Illness." *American Journal of Public Health* 57 (1967): 424-440.

Schelling, T. C. "The Life You Save May Be Your Own." In *Problems in Public Expenditure*, edited by S. Chase, 127-76. Washington, D.C.: Brookings Institution, 1968.

Schoenbaum, S. C., B. J. McNeill, and J. Kavet. "The Swine-Influenza Decision." *New England Journal of Medicine* 295 (1976): 759-765.

Schwartz, W. B., G. A. Gorry, J. P. Kassirer, and A. Essig. "Decision Analysis and Clinical Judgement." *American Journal of Medicine* 55 (1973): 459-472.

Stason, W. B., and M. C. Weinstein. "Allocation of Resources to Manage Hypertension." *New England Journal of Medicine* 296 (1977): 732-739.

Thaler, R., and S. Rosen. "The Value of Saving a Life: Evidence from the Labor Market." In *Household Production and Consumption*, edited by N. E. Terleckyj, 265-301. New York: National Bureau of Economic Research, 1976.

Torrency, G. W., D. L. Sackett, and W. H. Thomas. "Utility Maximization Model for Program Evaluation: A Demonstration Application." In *Health Status Indexes: Proceedings of a Conference Conducted by Health Services Research*, edited by R. L. Berg. Chicago: Hospital Research and Educational Trust, 1973.

Weinstein, M. C., and W. B. Stason. *Hypertension: A Policy Perspective*. Cambridge, Mass.: Harvard University Press, 1976.

Weisbrod, B. A. *Economics of Public Health: Measuring the Economic Impact of Diseases*. Philadelphia: University of Pennsylvania Press, 1961.

Zeckhauser, R. "Procedures for Valuing Lives." *Public Policy* 23 (1975): 419-464.

Cost-Effectiveness Methodologies for University Decisions

Fred Balderston, *University of California, Berkeley*

PURPOSE: LEVELS OF DECISION

The purpose of cost-effectiveness analysis is to help an institution and its leaders make wiser decisions. There are several possible levels of decision, and thus of analysis for cost-effectiveness. The broadest level encompasses decisions about policy and resources for an entire national society. An example of this is Secretary of Education Lamar Alexander's announcement that he will seek authority to change the criteria for awarding Pell grants to concentrate the available funds upon students coming from low-income families and to exclude middle-class students.

In the federal system of the United States, most important public funding and policy decisions for education are made at the state level. Currently preoccupying all those in California and Massachusetts public higher education are absolute reductions in state higher education appropriations for 1991-92. The amount and composition of these cuts will affect both state-funded financial assistance to students (thereby also affecting the demand for enrollment at the institutions that students choose to attend) and the public institutions whose budgets come wholly or in large part from state appropriations.

These two decision levels urgently require policy analysis as a basis for political argument and negotiations. In this chapter, however, we focus our main attention on the individual institution of higher education and its sub-units.

ACTIVITY ANALYSIS OF HIGHER EDUCATION

Analysis of results as compared with costs is easiest if the organization in question produces just one kind of result or output; if it uses only a single type of resource, at a well-defined price per unit; and if the output is produced in a short time and has immediate consequences. None of these three conditions holds for higher education institutions: They use many different kinds of resources; they produce many different kinds of results; the time required to earn a degree stretches over several years; and the value of that degree is usually realized over the working life of the student. Therefore, it is necessary to delineate the functions and sets of activities undertaken by the institution, in order to locate properly the decision problem that requires analysis and in order to have a framework from which to trace costs and effects.

The functions of a higher education institution are, in the conventional definition, to provide *instruction*, to conduct *research and scholarly activity*, and to undertake *community and public service*. A particular college or university has a particular mix of these functions, and this in turn directs its attention toward specific external constituencies and causes it to budget its professional and financial resources so as to perform its mix of functions in the most appropriate fashion.

Some administrative units are assigned to only one of these functional areas: For example, an organized research unit (ORU) in a research university is the locus of research programs in a particular field, and it does not offer courses of instruction. Other units have two or more basic functions: For example, an academic department offers courses for credit toward degrees, and it also supports the individual creative and scholarly activities of its faculty members and advanced students. Some faculty members may also engage in community service, teaching extension or non-credit courses or offering professional services through community organizations, and their academic department may be valued for this contribution as well.

In the 1960s and 1970s, techniques of program budgeting proved useful for governmental decision making at both federal and state levels, and they were applied to public higher education. Program budgeting reorganizes the data on resources used so as to align more explicitly each collection of resources with its use toward a defined programmatic purpose.

For each general mission of the organization, it is first necessary to define the objectives that are to be achieved. Then, the primary program that is dedicated to that mission is defined, and each type of resource used for it is identified and measured. In addition to primary or direct programs, a series of supporting programs is identified; the manager of a primary program relies on these for essential services. A university's library and its accounting and business services units are examples of supporting programs.

A planning, programming, budgeting system (PPBS) distinguishes among several time horizons: the long-range plan (usually more than five years), the programming interval (one to five years), and the budget period (one year). These are nested together and are tested for consistency (Hitch, 1965).

When carefully done with respect to a particular mission-directed program, the cost accounting approach can give a clearer picture of, for example, the "total cost of instruction" as against the "total cost of organized research."

While there are numerous analytical pitfalls, and the approach does not resolve some important dimensions of a major decision problem, it does help to develop structural linkages between resources used (inputs) and results achieved (outputs).

COST METHODOLOGIES: A PRELIMINARY VIEW

Cost Categories and Boundaries

An educational institution has a large number of buildings in its capital plant and numerous types of capital equipment. Typically, the institution's budget and its accounting structure are divided into its capital costs and its operating or ongoing costs. Capital costs assigned to a program or decision must usually be annualized during cost analysis so that full annual costs can be estimated. (It is an idiosyncrasy of college and university accounting that annual depreciation is not accounted for in the regular operating accounts. This tends to distort interpretation and decision making.)

Operating costs are incurred within the current period. One way of subdividing these is according to types of items in account classifications: salaries, operating supplies, utilities expense, etc. *Direct* costs are those clearly assignable to a particular department or activity. *Indirect* costs cover those activities or services that are shared among several departments or units.

Those costs arising within, and processed through, the institution's accounting system are within the boundaries for determination of institutional costs. But some cost analysis necessarily ignores or pierces the institutional boundary: For example, the student's cost of attendance for an academic year includes many items (books, transportation, off-campus rental and food, etc.) that are outside the institution's boundary, but important to estimate for such institutional purposes as the administration of student financial aid.

Constructed Cost Functions

In his well-known work on costs in higher education institutions, Howard Bowen constructed several functions for instructional costs (Bowen, 1980). A large lecture course, for example, needs a senior professor to lecture and a group of graduate student instructors (teaching assistants) to lead small discussion sections and to grade papers and examinations. A small seminar, on the other hand, has a different configuration of faculty input as well as a small enrollment. Bowen used these to discuss differences in institutional cost patterns.

Cost Accounting

The program budgeting approach mentioned above requires some reliance upon *cost accounting*.   This is one of the major methodologies for cost-effectiveness studies. It is used to trace where costs are absorbed, and for what purpose, in a situation where multiple inputs are used to engage in a sequence of activities or to produce multiple outputs. In the university setting, for example, the support function entitled "maintenance and operation of plant" (M&O) absorbs both personnel and nonpersonnel costs. The accounting system should be designed to provide directly the first cut of cost allocation, assigning to M&O the full salaries and benefits of those employees who work full time on M&O and the materials and services directly charged to M&O accounts. Beyond this, however, some personnel and other costs not directly charged to M&O accounts may actually be *partly* contributory to that function, and a cost-accounting analysis can show how much to reallocate into M&O.

Two or more functional activities are often served by the same employee or by a common support service. For example, a university's research library is drawn upon for instructional purposes, and the research organizations and their projects also us library services. In order to impute some library costs to research, cost accountants accumulate these costs into an aggregate pool. Then they may sample the circulation records to determine what percentage of usage comes from instructional sources and what percentage from personnel in the research organizations. Fractions of the cost pool are then assigned to research in accordance with the calculated percentages.

This sort of cost pooling and assignment in accordance with a usage variable is the basis for each component of the calculation of the indirect costs of research, and these are in turn the basis for the indirect cost recovery rate, or overhead rate that each university negotiates with federal research agencies. Cost accounting of this kind also provides a basis for full costing of specific university programs.

Statistical Cost Functions

An institution's costs of operation vary with its enrollment and with the composition of that enrollment. Overall variations of costs with enrollment can be estimated by performing a time-series regression with enrollment as the independent variable and cost as the dependent variable. The intercept would then represent fixed cost and the slope coefficient the variable cost per student. There are, of course, many possible difficulties with this approach.

A more intricate approach takes into account the fact that instructional costs vary according to class size and according to other course-related institutional

Table 5.1
Breakdowns and Percentages of Students in Each of the Categories of Total and Working Populations by Academic Level

Academic Level	TOTAL POPULATION			WORKING POPULATION		
	Non-Minority	Minority	All	Non-Minority	Minority	All
Freshman						
No. of Students	794	338	1,132	181	102	283
Percent/Total Students	70.9	29.9	100.0	64.0	36.0	100.0
Percent/Total Working				22.8	30.2	25.
No. of Dropouts	66	53	119	20	18	38
Percent/Total Students	8.3	15.7	10.5	11.0	17.6	13.4
Percent/Total Working				30.2	34.0	31.9
Sophomores						
No. of Students	1,319	302	1,621	411	160	571
Percent/Total Students	81.4	18.6	100.0	72.0	28.0	100.0
Percent/Total Working				31.2	53.0	35.2
No. of Dropouts	97	35	132	37	25	62
Percent/Total Students	7.4	11.6	8.1	9.0	15.6	10.9
Percent/Total Working				38.1	71.4	47.0
Juniors						
No. of Students	1,382	213	1,595	580	128	708
Percent/Total Students	86.6	13.4	7.7	81.9	18.1	100.0
Percent/Total Working				42.0	60.1	44.4
No. of Dropouts	103	20	123	51	13	64
Percent/Total Students	7.5	9.4	7.7	8.8	10.2	9.0
Percent/Total Working				49.5	65.0	52.0
Seniors						
No. of Students	1,732	169	1,901	928	117	1,045
Percent/Total Students	91.1	8.9	100.0	88.8	11.2	100.0
Percent/Total Working				53.6	69.2	55.0
No. of Dropouts	228	26	254	127	18	145
Percent/Total Students	13.2	15.4	13.4	13.7	15.4	13.9
Percent/Total Working				55.7	69.2	57.1

Source: Haigh, (1991).

Figure 5.1
Micro Model: Effects of Student Employment for the Individual while in College

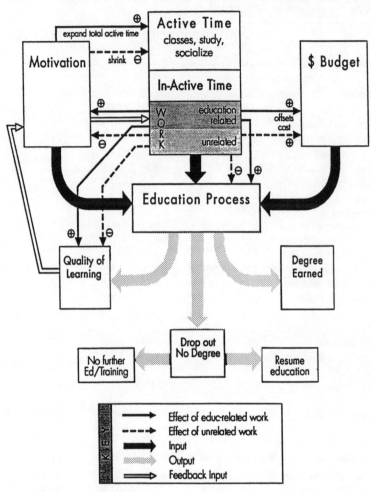

Source: Haigh (1991).

costs. An induced course-load matrix is first calculated, showing what distribution of courses the students in various majors have taken.

Cross-sectional study of cost patterns in several institutions is a third statistical approach. The instructional process requires several types of inputs, and it produces, as a quantitatively defined product, student credit hours, or degrees earned. Radner and Miller utilized econometric methods to estimate how close each institution in a sample was to the "efficient frontier" —that is, to achieving the largest possible results from the inputs it used.

EFFECTS, RESULTS, OUTPUTS

The *cost-effectiveness* of a program or a change in program can be assessed only if both its costs and its effects are evaluated. Defining and measuring these effects (or results or outputs) is often conceptually and practically more difficult than cost analysis. The short-term effects for the student include maturation, heightening of expectations and awareness of the society and culture, and job placement. There are also lifetime effects (e.g., getting started in a career for which the opportunity gateway is an appropriate education). A large amount of educational research has been devoted to sorting out and attempting to measure these short-term and long-term effects.

In institutional analysis, the volume of activity, not the significant effect or impact, is often measured. Thus, an institution measures student enrollment (head count or full-time equivalent), which is a volume-in-process measure. It can also assemble statistics of courses taken or student credit hours generated; these are "intermediate products", in the parlance of production systems. Counting the number of degrees granted of each type (B.A., B.S., M.A., M.S., M.B.A., J.D., Ph.D., etc.) comes closer to being a measure of results, though it says nothing about the content or quality of these degrees or their value to the individual and society.

Looking more deeply at the question of effects of an educational experience, the student brings into the educational process a certain level of native talent and of previous education. The education gained certainly adds *incrementally* to the student's capacities and value in employment or in creative citizenship. (It may even be "transforming" in the sense that the student's values, aspirations, and perspective on life are modified.) But the college or university would be ascribing undue credit to its own educational process if it simply counted its success stories without correcting for the contributions of the student's previous background and native talent to subsequent success.

Various sectors of the community and of the economy also receive effects from the institution's activities. On an immediate local basis, a sizeable college or university is an employer, and its students, as well as faculty, staff, and visitors, put purchasing power into the local economy.

Effects on labor markets and productivity are longer-term. Educated young people seek job placement, and they are expected not only to have professional qualifications (in engineering, accounting or other specialties) but to be well-motivated to learn their new jobs through training schemes.

A market-price characterization of the value of these educational effects would start with the increment of earnings that the college-educated young person would receive annually (as compared to earnings as a result of going directly to work without college) and then would discount all of the annual earnings increments back to the present. This—to continue a market-price evaluation—would then be compared with the expense of the education plus the opportunity cost of earnings foregone during the educational interval. Of course, other important effects and values are not captured by this narrowly defined measure of the economic gains attributable to education.

Economic and social sectors and society as a whole also benefit from the flow of new knowledge arising in basic and applied sciences. Universities contribute especially heavily through basic research programs. Their programmatic research in applied areas such as transportation engineering or international business may serve as a basis for significant improvements in technology and efficiency in both the public and the private sectors. Both basic and applied research feed into the process of innovation, which sustains real economic growth. (In this process, corporate enterprises concentrate most of their attention and resources on immediate applied research and on commercialization. These usually have the greatest market payoff.)

COST-EFFECTIVENESS: MATCHING COSTS AND EFFECTS

Examples may help to show how cost-effectiveness can be gauged.

Student Part-Time Work, and Degree Completion

Many undergraduate students in U.S. colleges and universities engage in part-time work during the academic year in order to meet part of their costs of education. This reduces the time available for study in formal courses and for the enjoyments of college life. One possible hazard, therefore, is that part-time work may increase the probability the will drop-out before completing of the college degree. Yet the official work-study programs of collegiate institutions (some with government funding) and the "student contribution" component of typical financial aid packaging both push students toward part-time employment.

In a 1991 doctoral dissertation, Cheryl Haigh investigated this question

(Haigh, 1991). Her conceptual model of the connections between student employment and other aspects of the educational process is reproduced in Figure 5.1. Haigh then assembled a uniquely suitable database from varied sources on the Berkeley campus and undertook extensive econometric modeling and estimation concerning the problem. The basic data, which were of the form shown in Table 5.1, permitted exploration of similarities or differences in persistence between nonminority students (including Asians) and minority students (African Americans, Hispanics, and Native Americans).

Haigh found that too many hours per week of employment had adverse effects upon grade-point average (GPA); off-campus employment or on-campus employment *in jobs unrelated to the student's major* had some negative effect on persistence. But employment for fifteen hours per week or less in *jobs related to the student's major* had a *positive* effect on GPA and persistence. In the exacting statistical testing leading to these results, Haigh utilized regression and probit models and sought to hold other factors constant while estimating the effect on persistence of each of the above variables. Of all the determinants of persistence, GPA was the most important single variable in this, as in other persistence studies; but the different effects on persistence of types of part-time work were also successfully measured.

Implications for student advising, financial aid administration, and university academic organization are quite strong. Colleges and universities should be wary of pushing students to do part-time work simply to earn the money to attend; but they should undertake pro-active programs to enlist students in academically related part-time on-campus employment.

In this example, the emphasis was not upon cost differences among alternatives—part-time off-campus work; part-time oncampus work unrelated to academic major; part-time on-campus work related to academic major—but upon impact differences. These were the different effects of these work experiences upon persistence toward the completion of the degree. An extensive database and powerful statistical tools were required to trace these impacts, with control over other variables that might also influence the effects. Only when this tracing was done could a preferred policy of financial aid administration be identified.

Budgeted Year-Round Operation of University of California Campuses

During the 1960s, the University of California (UC) projected rapid enrollment growth to meet its master plan obligation of providing entering undergraduate enrollment places for all California-resident applicants in the top 12.5 percent of the high school graduating class. Campus expansion to

Table 5.2
Comparison of Enrollments and Capacity of University of California General Campuses for 1970-1979

	Enrollments	Capacity[a]
1970-71[b]	98,29	97,637[c]
1971-72[b]	97,301	105,575
1972-73	100,301	105,400
1973-74	104,096	107,476
1974-75	108,700	113,190
1975-76	112,500	116,206
1976-77	115,100	119,944
1977-78	117,700	123,869
1978-79	120,400	128,040

[a] 1972-77 Capital Improvement Program as of August 27, 1971, subject to revision.

[b] Actual three-term average head count.

[c] All capacity numbers are three-term average head count and assume current discipline mix.

Source: Balderston and Weathersby, 1972-73, 50.

accommodate this growth was estimated to be very expensive to the state. The state government therefore pressed the university to schedule regular instruction during the summer months so that the "throughput" of students receiving and completing their education would be increased without so much capital expenditure for expanded facilities. Projections of the enrollment and the capacity of UC campuses, 1970-79, are shown in Table 5.2. Table 5.3 summarizes classroom utilization rates under alternative class-hour schedules, an important determinant of the enrollment-absorbing capability of classroom space; these figures were derived from a simulation study of scheduling alternatives. Enrollment patterns are shown for two growth models in Figures 5.2, 5.3, and 5.4.

Students, however, traditionally prefer the fall/spring academic year. In the absence of outright compulsory summer-term attendance, they would enroll for a summer term in smaller numbers than they would for the fall or spring semester (see Figure 5.5.) The decline in average class size during a summer term would then affect instructional costs per student. It would also be sensible to shift from a semester calendar to a quarter calendar in order to equalize the length of the summer term with the length of other terms. Figure 5.6 then shows the critical class-size region for which equal or equivalent costs of operation would be achieved; the Summer quarter has a cost advantage if class sizes do not decline very much, but at larger percentage declines, the traditional two-semester plan is more cost-effective.

Table 5.3
**Summary of Classroom Utilization Rates, Assignable Square Feet, and Variable
Costs for Ten-Year Runs (1969-70 to 1978-79) Using Data from the University of
California at Santa Barbara**

Performance Measurement (1)	Starting with Actual Fall 1969 Inventory			
	Lumpy Schedule[a]		Flat Schedule[b]	
	67-Hr. Week (Run 10A) (2)	44-Hr. Week (Run 12B) (3)	67-Hr. Week (Run 11A) (4)	44-Hr. Week (Run 12A) (5)
Classroom Utilization (Ave. in the 10 years)				
Weekly Rm. Hrs. per Room	30.5	30.3	32.9	31.3
Station Occupancy	0.50[b]	0.48[b]	0.52[b]	0.47[b]
Weekly Student Hours Per Station	15.4	14.5	16.9	14.8
Assignable Sq. Ft. per WSH	**0.87**	**0.91**	**0.82**	**0.90**
Assignable Sq. Ft. in the 10th Year (thous.)				
Classrooms	127.0	136.0	119.0	133.01
Class Labs	229.0	225.0	212.0	221.0
All Other Instruction & Resource (I&R)	535.0	537.0	544.0	539.0
Total I&R Facilities	**891.0**	**898.0**	**875.0**	**893.0**
Total Variable Costs in the 10 years (mil.)				
Salaries & Support	$ 145.3	$ 147.4	$ 152.2	$ 148.6
Maintenance & Operation of Plant	17.6	17.7	17.4	17.47
Debt Service[c]	16.8	17.1	15.9	17.1
Total Variable Costs	**$ 179.7**	**$ 182.2**	**$ 185.5**	**$ 183.4**

[a] "Lumpy" = varying numbers of classes in different hours, as in actual schedules. "Flat" = as nearly equal numbers of classes in all hours as is possible.
[b] 0.60 to 0.75 in most room-size ranges, but the overall ratio is reduced by the disproportionate effect of a few very large rooms.
[c] For bonds by which construction is assumed to financed.

Source: Balderston and Weathersby (1972-73, 51).

Table 5.4
Critical Class-Size Values for Cost Equality between Semester System and Quarter System Operating under Model 1

Ratio of 4th Quarter FTE Enrollment (y) / 3 Term Aver. FTE Enrollment	Percent Decline in Class Size
1.00	13%
0.80	13
0.60	13
0.40	12
0.20	10

Source: Balderston & Weathersby (1972-73).

Table 5.5
Table of ƒ Factors Describing Economies of Scale for Summer Quarter Support Operations

Functional Form	Numeric Value
Constant	1.0 0.8 0.6 0.4 0.5
Linear	$f = y$ $y = (0.2, 0.4, 0.6, 0.8, 1.0)$
Log-Parabolic	$f = 15.4\,y^2$ $\quad\quad\quad y \leq .18$ $f = .328 + .672 \log(10y)\ y \leq .18$

Source: Balderston & Weathersby (1972-73).

The university did begin quarter-system calendars and a full summer quarter, commencing in 1966. But by 1970 there was a reversal of policy, and the State determined that it would not fund the summer quarter as a regular quarter. Earlier studies of the attractiveness of year-round operation (YRO) had assumed that campuses were not utilized during the summer months; but, in fact, fee-based summer sessions at major campuses did enroll significant numbers of regular students who wanted to speed up their progress toward degrees. This enrollment did not have a budgeted instructional cost in the university's state-funded budget. Furthermore, the earlier projections of rapid enrollment growth (at rates up to 10 percent per year) proved wrong. Fee increases dampened enrollment demand, and in-migration to California slowed

Figure 5.2
Model 1: Entire System Enrollment Pattern

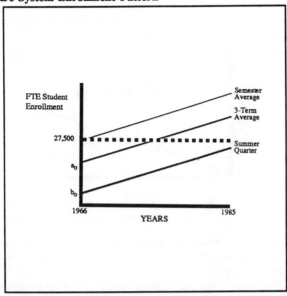

Figure 5.2 increases total student enrollment at a constant rate beginning at 27,500 FTE. The semester system (top line) immediately exceeds the current enrollment; under the quarter system (bottom two lines) the three term enrollment immediately falls to a_0 and grows steadily, while summer quarter enrollment begins at b_0 and grows at the same rate. The ratio of b_0 to a_0 is defined as y and describes the percent the summer quarter is of three-term enrollment (Balderston and Weathersby, 1972-73, 54).

down. Enrollment growth at the university slowed to 1 percent per year. The combination of these factors was such that YRO failed to be cost-effective.

Academic Research

Research and creative scholarship are part of the mission of the major universities, and research achievement is an employment obligation of the faculty members. These universities devote a significant portion of their own budgeted resources to research libraries, laboratory facilities, and operating support of research. In addition, faculty members and organized research units (ORUs), especially in the sciences, engineering, and biomedical fields, seek extramural research grants and contracts. The modes of organization of university research are discussed in detail elsewhere (Balderston, 1990).

Figure 5.3
Model 2: Growing Campuses Enrollment Pattern

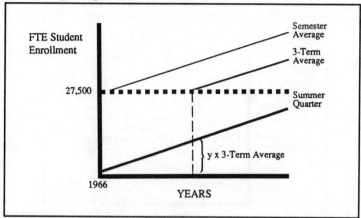

Figure 5.3 also increases total student enrollment at a constant rate beginning at 27,500 FTE. The semester system (top line) is the same as in Figure 5.2. However, unlike Figure 5.2, Figure 5.3 accommodates all the growth in total FTE enrollment in the summer quarter until the summer quarter enrollment is $y\%$ of the three-term enrollment from which time they both grow at the same rate (Balderston and Weathersby, 1972-73, 56).

Figure 5.4
Model 3: Mature Campuses Enrollment Pattern

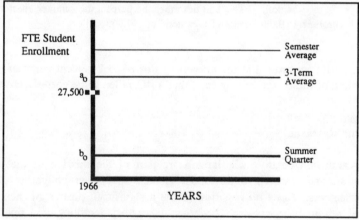

Figure 5.4 describes a one-time change in total enrollment which is then constant into the future. The same total enrollment is accommodated in both the semester and the quarter systems with the ratio $b_0/a_0 = y$ (Balderston and Weathersby, 1972-72, 57).

Figure 5.5
Plot of *S*-Curve Function Showing Economies of Scale in Summer Quarter Support Operations

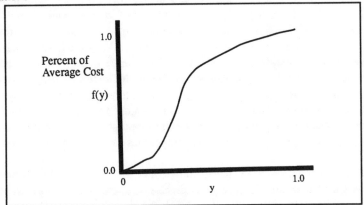

The mathematical expression in Table 5.4 describes the *S*-shaped curve shown above. For proportionately small summer enrollments (low values of *y*), the cost of summer quarter support operations would be proportionately small (low values of *f*). When summer quarter enrollments are as great as three-term averages support costs in the summer would be the same as in the regular terms (Balderston and Weathersby, 1972-73, 58).

Figure 5.6
Critical Class-Size Region for Cost Equality between Semester System and Quarter System Operating under Figures 5.3 and 5.4

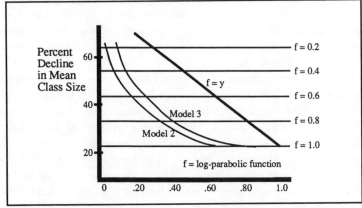

The region below the *f*-function curves shown above describes the relative economic advantage of the four-quarter year-round system. In the region above the *f*-function curves the two-semester system would possess the relative economic advantage.

When faculty members achieve and report results, their peers in the discipline evaluate the quality of their work. Path-breaking results are cited frequently in the scholarly literature, and universities now use citation indexes as one measure of the significance and quality of achievement. The faculty member has the rewards of reputation, advancement, and greater future research support, and the university's reputation is enhanced. Winning in the competition for reputation is a major operational payoff for universities from excellence in basic research. The 1982 *Assessment of Research-Doctorate Programs in the United States* (Jones, Linzey & Coggeshall) captures many of the impacts of sustained expenditure and striving in the major academic disciplines and engineering fields. Aggressive efforts to build reputation in a field do take time, and even with large expenditures they sometimes fail to impress the scholarly community.

In the sciences, cumulative knowledge is relied on by researchers everywhere so that beneficial impacts diffuse throughout the world. In applied science and engineering, on the other hand, the specific impacts of research are more readily evaluated. Agricultural research has resulted in improved plant and animal varieties, better pest control, protection of the land, and labor saving. In the United States, land-grant universities contribute greatly to research achievements through their agricultural experiment stations and their networks of field agents; funding comes from federal, state and private sources. Selected productivity measures and expenditure patterns for agricultural research are shown in Figures 5.7 and 5.8., respectively. The benefits and long-term rates of return of agricultural research are summarized in Table 5.6. This study of agricultural research also distinguished between science-oriented and technology-oriented research, the latter having the direct objective of producing new technology. Both types of agricultural research are, for the most part, conducted together. The imputed rates of return are very high, with recent science-oriented research showing a somewhat lower rate of return than does technology-oriented research.

Widely varying conditions in the United States necessitate a decentralized, state-by-state approach to this applied research. A question then arises whether the sponsoring state captures the benefits, or whether there is leakage of the productivity gains to other places. The right-most column of Table 5.6 shows that the local benefit of technology generally exceeds 50 percent of total productivity change, whereas (as one would suspect) science-oriented research diffuses more readily to other places. These findings have helped to make the case for continued significant public funding of agricultural research. Productivity advances usually translate relatively quickly into consumer-level prices of food and fiber. As agribusiness entities increase in size and profitability, however, political pressures arise to require more private support of this research.

Figure 5.7
Productivity Measures (1967 = 100)

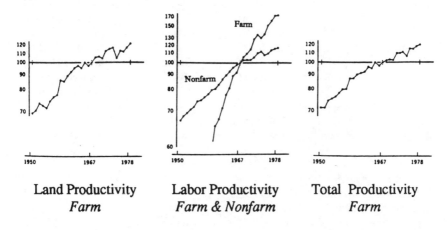

Land Productivity	Labor Productivity	Total Productivity
Farm	*Farm & Nonfarm*	*Farm*

Figure 5.8
Expenditures (in 1967 Dollars) of State Stations and USDA on Research on Sixteen Products as a Function of the Gross Income for the Product in 1975

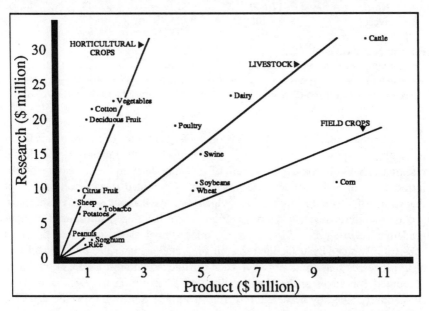

Source: Evenson, Waggoner & Ruttan (1979, 1105).   Copyright 1979 by the AAAS.

Table 5.6
Percentage of Productivity Change Realized in the State Undertaking the Research

Subject	Maximum Annual Benefit from $1000 Investment (dollars)	Annual Rate of Return (%)	Percentage of Productivity Change Realized in the State Undertaking the Research
	1868 to 1926		
All agricultural research	12,500	65	Not estimated
	1927 to 1950		
Agricultural research			
Technology-oriented	11,400	95	55
Science-oriented	53,000	110	33
	1948 to 1971		
Agricultural research			
Technology-oriented			
South	21,000	130	67
North	11,600	93	43
West	12,200	95	67
Science-oriented	4,500	45	32
Farm management and			
agricultural extension	2,173	110	100

Source Evenson, Waggoner & Ruttan (1979, 1105). Copyright 1979 by the AAAS.

A similar attempt to focus upon productivity and rates of return of academic research is reported by Mansfield (1991) for seven industries. Academic research is held to produce the benefit of reducing delay in the development and introduction of new products and processes. Computed rates of return reflect the value of this delay reduction, which averages about seven years. New products in these seven industries that could not have been introduced without academic research had $24 billion in total annual sales, and new products substantially aided by academic research generated annual sales of $17.1 billion. New processes that could not have been introduced without academic research accounted for an estimated total savings of $7.2 billion in 1985, and those substantially aided by academic research saved $11.3 billion (Mansfield, 1991, p. 4).

Mansfield computed social rates of return for academic research, using a number of plausible assumptions. Tabular information from his 1991 article shows a range of rates of return under differing definitions. Mansfield employs the conservative assumption that at least one-half of the new products and processes adopted would not have been developed or would have been greatly delayed without the help of academic research. The highest rate of return, 28 percent, includes benefits to users from new products; but excluding these benefits, the rate of return is still a respectable 10 percent (Mansfield, 1991, p. 11).

The federal research-funding agencies, and the universities, can use these findings to buttress their case for continued high budgetary support for academic research. These findings do not, however, provide guidance on the interesting problems of conducting research projects for the greatest payoff in relation to cost. That is a significant problem of a very different sort. The researcher or research administrator faces deep uncertainties regarding the timing and the content of discovery, plus the frequent necessity to link a series of discoveries if a market-valued innovation is to occur. The challenges of cost-effective research project management deserve a full discussion on another day.

NOTE

This chapter was prepared for TechnoServe's National Workshop on Cost-Effectiveness in the Nonprofit Sector held at Stanford University June 27-28, 1991.

REFERENCES

Balderston, Frederick E. *Managing Today's University*. Cambridge, Mass.: Ballinger, 1974.

Balderston, Frederick E. "Organization, Funding, Incentives and Initiatives for University Research: A University Management Perspective." In *The Economics of American Universities*, edited by Stephen A. Hoenack and Eileen L. Collins, 33-52. Albany, N.Y.: SUNY Press, 1990.

Balderston, Frederick E., and George B. Weathersby, "PPBS in Higher Education Planning and Management." Parts 1-3, *Higher Education* 1, no. 2; 1, no.3; 2, no.1, 1972-73.

Bowman, Margaret, Jorge Baanante, Thomas Dichter, Steven Londner, and Peter Reiling. *Measuring Our Impact: Determining Cost-Effectiveness of Non-governmental Organization Development Projects*. Norwalk, Conn.: TechnoServe, 1989.

Dorfman, Robert, ed. *Measuring Benefits of Government Investments*. Washington, D.C.: The Brookings Institution, 1965.

Evenson, Robert E., Paul E. Waggoner, and Vernon W. Ruttan. "Economic Benefits from Research: An Example from Agriculture." *Science* 205 (September 1979): 1104-1105.

Haigh, Cheryl L. "Employment While in College: A Study of Its Effect on Academic Achievement and Persistence at a Major University." Ph.D. diss., University of California, Berkeley, 1991.

Hitch, Charles J. *Decision-Making for Defense*. Los Angeles: University of California Press, 1965.

Jones, Lyle V., Gardner Lindzey, and Porter E. Coggeshall, eds. *An Assessment of Research-Doctorate Programs in the United States*. 5 vols. Washington, D.C.: National Academy Press, 1982. 5 vols.

Kogan, Maurice, ed. *Evaluating Higher Education*. London: Jessica Kingsley, 1989.

Levin, Henry M. *Cost-Effectiveness: A Primer*. Beverly Hills: Sage Publications, 1983.

Mansfield, Edwin. "Academic Research and Industrial Innovation." *Research Policy* 20 (1991): 1-12.

Mishan, E. J. *Cost-Benefit Analysis*. New York: Praeger, 1976.

U.S. Department of Education, Office of Educational Research and Improvement. *Price and Quality in Higher Education*. Washington, D.C.: U.S. Government Printing Office, 1990.

Woodhall, Maureen. *Cost-Benefit Analysis in Educational Planning*. Paris: International Institute for Educational Planning, 1970.

6

The Cycle of Cost-Effectiveness: The Nature Conservancy

Eric Halperin and Leslie A. Williams,
The Nature Conservancy
Rebecca Paxton Stewart, *TechnoServe, Inc.*

At The Nature Conservancy, cost-effectiveness is built into our management system. In order to understand how this works, it is helpful to get acquainted first with the general purpose, structure and operations of the Conservancy.

The Nature Conservancy preserves plants, animals, and natural communities that represent the diversity of life on earth by protecting the lands and waters that they need to survive. Owning and managing the largest private system of nature sanctuaries in the world, over the past forty years the Conservancy has preserved more that 5.4 million acres in the United States and more than 15 million acres in Latin American, the Caribbean, and the Pacific Rim.

The Conservancy works by:

- *Identifying* lands that shelter the best examples of natural communities and species; determining what is truly rare and where it exists.

- *Protecting* habitats and natural systems through acquisition by gift or purchase; assisting government and other conservation organizations in their land preservation efforts.

- *Managing* more than 1,600 preserves using staff and volunteer land stewards encouraging compatible use of the sanctuaries by researchers, students, and the public.

ORGANIZATION

The Nature Conservancy was incorporated in 1951 for scientific and educational purposes. It is a nonprofit, tax-exempt corporation under section 501(c)3 of the Internal Revenue Code and is a publicly supported organization as defined in sections 170(b)(1)(vi) and 509(a). The Conservancy's activities are made possible through individual and corporate contributions, foundation grants, membership dues, and recovery of expenses.

The Conservancy has an open membership policy and an elected Board of

Figure 6.1
Level of Endangerment—Global

LEVEL   DEFINITION

G1   Critically imperiled globally
G2   Imperiled globally
G3   Rare or uncommon but not imperiled
G4   Not rare and apparently secure, but with long-term cause
        for concern
G5   Demonstrably widespread, abundant and secure
GH   Of historical occurrence, possibly extinct
GX   Presumed extinct

Figure 6.2
Level of Endangerment—State

LEVEL   DEFINITION

S1   Critically imperiled within the state
S2   Imperiled within the state
S3   Rare or uncommon but not imperiled
S4   Not rare and apparently secure, but with long-term cause
        for concern
S5   Demonstrably widespread, abundant and secure
SH   Of historical occurrence, possibly extinct
SX   Presumed extinct

Governors. In addition to its volunteers, the Conservancy employs over 1,200 professional staff members with backgrounds ranging from systems ecology, biology, and forestry to real estate, business, and law.

The Conservancy's headquarters are located in metropolitan Washington, D.C. The same building also houses the headquarters of the International Program. Professionally staffed offices are located in all fifty states.

The Nature Conservancy has expanded its program to encompass areas outside the United States. The Pacific program, headquartered in Hawaii, is working to identify and protect threatened areas in Indonesia, Melanesia, and

Micronesia. In Latin America, the Conservancy has joined forces with over thirty organizations covering seventeen countries in order to provide infrastructure, community development, professional training, and long-term funding for legally protected, but under funded, areas throughout the continent.

The Conservancy attracted more than $136 million in 1991, which represents roughly one-third of the private funding donated to national environmental groups in the United States in that year. In addition, it also helped direct an equally large sum from government toward natural areas conservation. The actions of the Conservancy have helped inspire the creation of state government biological inventory and natural area programs and have contributed to the growth of land trusts and other conservation organizations.

The following describes in greater detail the primary functions of The Nature Conservancy. Defining these functions is the first step in the Conservancy's efforts to measure cost-effectiveness. It serves as the basis for assessing potential benefits from alternative actions and for judging results.

Identification

State Natural Heritage Inventory Programs, an invention of the Conservancy, are designed to produce ongoing inventories of natural elements and their locations within a particular state. The scientific information gathered by each inventory indicates the relative rarity of plant and animal species, aquatic and plant communities, and other significant ecological features. This systematic inventory process also indicates which natural elements are currently protected and which are not. Consequently, the data can be useful in guiding development citing decisions, in planning resource use, and in carrying out many other conservation initiatives.

As depicted in Figures 6.1 and 6.2, a rating system, developed by The Nature Conservancy in partnership with the various state Natural Heritage Inventory Programs, is used to measure the degree of threat to a particular plant or animal species. The ratings are applicable on both the state and the global levels, allowing a combination of the two (e.g., G3S2) to provide a more accurate portrait of the species' priority.

A strategy that has been invaluable in the success of the Heritage endeavor has been the Conservancy's use of "leverage" to multiply its investment in this program. Specifically, while the vast majority of Heritage Programs are now run by state agencies, *all* of them began as Nature Conservancy programs. Funds were invested in training, staff, computer equipment, and so on, while, at the same time, state funding was being pursued to make the Heritage Program a permanent institution within the state. Once state funding was secured, the Conservancy then moved to other states to replicate the process. State Heritage

Programs have now been established in all fifty states. Efforts on the domestic level have shifted to working with federal agencies, such as the U.S. Forest Service, and quasi-governmental entities, such as the Navajo Nation, to similarly institutionalize the Heritage Program methodology and data collection practices. A parallel effort, in which the Heritage Programs are referred to as Conservation Data Centers, has been under way in the past few years to implement the strategy worldwide. Initial efforts have focused on Latin America, Canada, and the Pacific Rim countries.

Protection

A project is undertaken on the basis of

- Heritage Program information that identifies a specific site sheltering critically threatened plant or animal species/communities or
- An acquisition strategy designed to enlarge an existing sanctuary according to priorities indicated by a Heritage Program.

The project is first reviewed by members of the Conservancy's management. If it clearly supports the Conservancy's mission, an appropriate protection strategy is developed and implemented. The Conservancy employs a host of protection techniques, including direct fee acquisitions, conservation easements, and voluntary landowner agreements. The Conservancy also works with a variety of public and private partners to protect critically endangered lands.

If funds are required to protect the site, upon approval, money for purchase is made available from the Conservancy's revolving Land Preservation Fund. The state chapter or special committee then raises funds to repay the Conservancy so that the money can be reinvested in other protection projects.

The Conservancy's efforts have had an important impact on biological diversity, particularly in the East and Midwest, where 45 percent of the G1 and G2 species (those found in less than twenty locations worldwide) have received Conservancy protection. Of the species rated G1 and G2 nationally, 20 percent have been protected.

Stewardship

The Conservancy's stewardship staff and volunteers maintain more than 1,600 preserves and employ such techniques prescribed burnings, reforestation, and fencing that both maintain the preserves and encourage the growth of endangered plants and animals that live within the preserves. These preserves range in size from less than one acre to more than 342,000 acres. Actual management is carried out by the volunteer committees and professional staff after a long-term management plan has identified stewardship needs. Most Conservancy preserves are open for educational uses and recreation such as hiking, nature study, bird watching, and photography.

Statistics

Acres saved in the United States since 1953	5.57 million
Acres managed	1.32 million
Membership	628,000
Preserves under Conservancy Management[1]	1,600
Natural Heritage Inventory Programs and Conservation Data Centers	82

New Initiatives

The Last Great Places Campaign seeks to forge an alliance for people and the environment. Its goal is to work with local communities to protect entire ecosystems, not just isolated islands of biodiversity. On May 14, 1991, The Nature Conservancy, in conjunction with more than one hundred public- and private-sector partners, unveiled a dozen on-the-ground, working models for large-scale ecosystem conservation throughout the Western Hemisphere. These diverse projects will demonstrate that the protection of functioning ecosystems in order to preserve species diversity can accommodate human economic and cultural needs as well.

The twelve models represent projects in various stages of development and experimentation; some having been quietly in the works for more than a decade. Although each is unique, all adhere to a basic design rationale of establishing strictly protected core natural areas surrounded by buffer zones, where appropriate human activities are encouraged. Besides providing economic and cultural benefits, these human activities are designed to be protection tools as well.

The projects unveiled represent what many consider to be the future of large-scale conservation worldwide. Noel Brown, director of the United Nations Environment Programme, states that the U.N. and other international bodies have proposed such an approach to conservation for some time. He continues to say that this is the first time such theories have been applied in practice by major conservation organization in a systematic way to such a diversity of ecosystems, tropical and temperate.

These models, dubbed "bioreserves" by Conservancy scientists, run the gamut from tall grass prairies to barrier islands, desert river systems, tropical rainforests, and near-urban watersheds. Similarly, the human endeavors being tested in the bioreserve buffer zones include farming, grazing, ecotourism, and even low-density housing and mineral extraction. Likewise, the diversity of partnerships being built to undertake such massive efforts encompasses all sectors of society—from nonprofit groups, corporations, and universities to local, state, and federal agencies, civic organizations, and scores of private individuals and landowners.

The bioreserve concept evolved over many years and was formalized after the Conservancy implemented an extensive strategic planning process. Analysis shows that, while much more needs to be done, strides have been made in identifying and protecting specific rare species' habitats. But little has been done to safeguard the larger landscapes these species need to survive.

An example of what caused the Conservancy to take the lead in this arena is the Virginia Coast Reserve, a string of fourteen barrier islands the Conservancy began acquiring in the 1970s. The initial motivation was to save some of the last Atlantic coastal habitat for increasingly rare shorebirds, waterfowl, and other native species. As development pressures mounted on the mainland, it became apparent that these fragile offshore islands would be adversely affected. Furthermore, unplanned growth might degrade the waters crucial to both a viable shorebird habitat and a healthy seafood industry—a mainstay of the local economy.

Drawing on research conducted by the University of Virginia and others on ground water and surface water pollution, the only viable solution was to encourage proper uses in a buffer zone sufficient to protect the island and coastal waters from the effects of adverse mainland development. Within the buffer zone, farming will continue in a manner that minimizes erosion and pollution. Traditional shellfish harvesting techniques similarly will continue, and low-density residential housing, planned in cooperation with local community groups and other relevant parties, will contrast with the nonbuffer high-density development already spreading from the Chesapeake Bay side of the Delmarva Peninsula. Conservation easements on certain key properties will help to make the buffer permanent.

The twelve models unveiled represent the future of Nature Conservancy action. Many more bioreserve projects are in the planning stages throughout the United States. Those in Latin America are being undertaken within the Conservancy's Parks in Peril Program, which seeks to build in-country infrastructure for the real protection of 200 critical protected areas in Central and South America and the Caribbean—areas that have been designated "parks" on a map, but that lack the staff, training, facilities, and financial support to realize true protection.

The twelve Last Great Places bioreserve sites are:

- Big Darby Watershed, Ohio
- Tallgrass Prairie Preserve, Oklahoma
- Nipomo Dunes, California
- Virginia Coast Reserve
- Peconic/Block Island, New York/Rhode Island
- Rio Celestun/Rio Lagartos, Mexico

- The Florida Keys
- Texas Hill Country
- Mbaracayu, Paraguay
- The Darien, Panama
- Southwest Ecosystems, Arizona/New Mexico
- Condor Reserve, Ecuador

THE METHODOLOGY, APPLICATION, AND HISTORY OF COST-EFFECTIVENESS

The Nature Conservancy's interest in cost-effectiveness is the result of a dedication to achieving its mission and a recognition that time to achieve that mission is running short. Its actions, strategies, and everyday decisions are all motivated by these factors, with cost-effectiveness being viewed by the Conservancy as a requirement, rather than an option, under these circumstances. The sections below offer examples and descriptions of how this cost-effectiveness manifests itself at the Conservancy.

The Nature Conservancy employs a multifaceted approach to controlling, measuring, and evaluating its cost-effectiveness. In sum, this approach emphasizes planning and feedback as its cornerstones. It begins with long-term and annual strategic planning—both on the national level and on the individual program, department, and office levels. This planning effort is itself directly tied into the Conservancy's budgeting process. To complete the circle, individual policies and procedures are used to amplify and accentuate these general organizational approaches to produce cost-effective behavior on a day-to-day basis. This process is illustrated in Figure 6.3.

As shown in Figure 6.3, the methodology utilizes all aspects of management and decision making. Each element of the cycle relies on the feedback of the others to evaluate its position relative to the goal. Alterations are made within each element to further ensure cost-effectiveness. The following is a description of how each facet is utilized and maneuvered to meet the needs of a changing environment.

Figure 6.3
The Nature Conservancy's Approach to Cost-Effectiveness

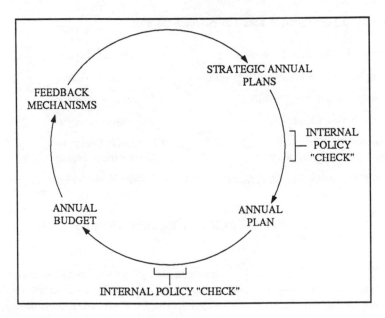

Strategic Planning

Biodiversity Rating

To ensure cost-effectiveness, the Conservancy's strategic plan mandates that the organization take new steps to focus its resources on the most biologically significant projects. For example, in selecting bioreserve sites, considerable weight is attached to their biological significance. The plan also calls for the use of evaluation tools, the Land Preservation Fund (LPF) guidelines, and other management tools to minimize spending on sites that either have lower biological significance or can be effectively protected by others. The plan encourages only projects that meet at least the criteria for a B3 biological rating (see Figure 6.4). In some cases, the plan highlights that this will mean identifying partners, such as local land trusts and public land conservation agencies, that can assume the lead in protecting other sites.

The tie to cost-effectiveness through strategic planning is further illustrated in the following two discussions taken from the Conservancy's latest strategic plan—one on its bioreserve initiative, and the second on its international efforts.

The cost-effectiveness of our mission can only be ensured if the viability of previously secured areas is protected from the impending breakdown of the larger areas on which they depend. This view is supported by our experience, and by studies which suggest that, all variables being equal, large areas provide more secure protection for species than small areas. In addition, we have found that focusing solely on core protected areas—even large areas—will not be sufficient to preserve biological diversity unless we address potentially incompatible human activities in the surrounding landscape. We can no longer ignore the actions of our neighbors and are faced with the job of influencing their activity. Each large ecosystem project is likely to require a level of capital investment and operating cost that go beyond what the Conservancy has historically devoted to individual projects, yet these investments must be made.

At the same time that we are faced with the challenge of protecting larger ecological systems, significant work remains to place rare and endangered elements under some form of protection. While lacking information on natural communities and other measures of biological diversity, Heritage information does show the number of G1 and G2 species (those found in less than 20 locations worldwide) potentially embraced by 74 major ecological systems in the U.S. Working on only these sites would leave a substantial portion of the nation's biodiversity unprotected.

One possible response is to ensure that the Conservancy focuses its efforts on those projects with the most biological significance. In fiscal year 1990 the Conservancy devoted 26 percent of acquisition funds to projects with less ecological significance. Although this percentage is relatively small, it could provide the Conservancy flexibility to redirect resources toward projects of the highest biological importance.

Bioreserves should be viewed as strategy within our mission of protecting biodiversity. It is an especially powerful strategy which we believe will (1) protect highly important natural systems; (2) boost the protection of all biodiversity by demonstrating that long-term viability of natural landscapes is achievable; and (3) broaden our skills, produce increased capital, and foster greater societal support for conservation. The "Last Great Places" Alliance is key to our bioreserve commitment.

The investments made thus far in our non-governmental organization (NGO) program have produced returns which far outweigh original costs. The Nature Conservancy has played an important role in the development of these NGOs—assisting in planning, training personnel, providing salaries for key personnel during the start-up phase, assisting on an ongoing basis with fundraising, and providing funding where appropriate. In Venezuela, for example, Bioma, a local NGO, helped design and persuaded the government to decree two major parks which contain significant biological diversity. Bioma is deeply involved in the management of these parks today. Fundacion Natura, another local NGO, has played a similar role in the creation of the Utria National Park in Colombia.

The key questions today deal with the long-term viability of our NGO partners. The circumstances under which conservation organizations are operating in Latin America—the relative poverty and political instability—create special challenges. Bioma, for example, has grown rapidly since its establishment in 1986. It has a staff of approximately 40 people and a 1990 budget of about $900,000. However, this rapid staff growth, combined with the expiration of key start-up grants, has made it difficult for the organization to fund its ongoing operations. Thus, Bioma was recently forced to lay off 20 percent of its staff. This seriously impedes the progress of the Conservancy's mission.

Figure 6.4
Biodiversity Rating

RATING DEFINITION

B1 Outstanding significance, such as only known occurrence of
    any element, best occurrences of G1 elements, or outstanding
    concentration of G1 or G2 elements. Viable and defensible
    site.

B2 Very high significance, such as best occurrences of G1
    elements or single most outstanding occurrence of G2, G3, or
    community elements.

B3 High significance, such as marginal occurrences of G2 or G3
    elements, excellent occurrences of any community element,
    or concentrations of S1 elements.

B4 Moderate significance, such as excellent occurrences of S1
    elements.

The primary means of addressing this situation is through the general fund
and the capital campaign. The Conservancy, in response to the goals of the
Annual Plan, has reviewed the ways in which sources of funds such as
membership dues, cash generated by unrestricted tradelands gifts, and
unrestricted bequests are allocated. These sources, which are not designated by
donors for particular programs, were previously allocated with only small weight
given to relative program need. Policies have been instituted to increase the
funds available for allocation. Newly drafted criteria for state program
evaluations provide incentives for generating resources for other needy areas.

On the international front, our work is relatively new. Its progress is
difficult to measure through simple yardsticks such as "acres protected," yet it
is increasingly important to communicate the impact of international work to the
rest of the organization. The Latin American Division's cost-effectiveness
assessment will include the development of detailed evaluations of the
effectiveness of each of its country programs. Similar evaluation will
specifically address the likely investment that the Conservancy should expect to
make in each of its country partners, and the impact of that investment. The
Latin American Division will also consider mechanisms to make these programs
as financially viable as possible. These same standards will then apply to the
Pacific program and any other new international initiatives.

Annual Planning/Budgeting

Annual planning and budgeting comprises the second central component of the Conservancy's approach to achieving cost-effectiveness. These two concepts are viewed as a dynamic, interwoven set of processes, which allows the Conservancy to achieve a number of important objectives:

- It allows management to chart the future course and direction of the organization.

- It serves as a current and historical benchmark that can be used to assess the Conservancy's performance and progress.

- It allows the Conservancy to make well-informed course and direction changes if situations warrant.

More specific aspects of the annual planning and budgeting process are given in the following sections.

Annual Planning

Emphasis on planning is The Nature Conservancy's most frequently acknowledged strength. Already mentioned was the long-range or strategic plan, which sets the overall course of the Conservancy's activities for the future. In contrast, the annual plan, required from each Conservancy operating entity, sets the more specific agenda for the organization's anticipated activities over the coming year.

The annual planning process, begins at headquarters where the Chief Operating Officer, who supervises the process, compiles a listing of organizational priorities for the coming year. In the field, detailed plans for state programs and preserves are then prepared. The region reviews and approves the plans from state offices and then incorporates all of the plans into a regional plan.

Department and program managers at headquarters simultaneously draft plans that complement the regional and state plans and that establish national priorities. Regional plans and departmental plans are reviewed at headquarters and are approved as the basis of the overall annual operating plan for the Conservancy.

At the state level, plans are developed jointly by the staff and chapter trustees. Simultaneously, state program staff consult with regional program staff to ensure that stewardship and other goals are carefully developed. Plans and budgets from state and local offices in most cases are first approved by their state or local chapter before submission to the regional office.

Field offices that supervise staffed preserves also coordinate the preparation of preserve plans and budgets with preserve staff committees. The divisional manager is responsible for monitoring the progress of each preserve's annual plan and for directing the preserve manager to modify/adjust the plan as circumstances change throughout the year.

Budgeting

Budgets are the financial representation of the planning process. The intent of budgeting at the Conservancy is to give more specific direction and to assist management in making the most productive and profitable use of the organization's limited resources.

The Finance Department is responsible for coordinating the budget process and supplying to departments/divisions the budget preparation package with the preliminary corporate plan, operating policies, and statistical data. Each department/division is responsible for preparing an individual plan and budget. The Finance Department then combines these plans and budgets to form the corporate plan and budget. Senior management reviews this complete plan and budget and then submits it to the Board of Governors for final approval at its annual June meeting.

Internal Feedback Mechanisms: Living Cost-Effectively

In order to remain cost-effective, The Nature Conservancy has generated a checks-and-balance system controlled by guidelines and procedures. The following policies and guidelines describe this concept further.

Loan Policies and Procedures

In order to achieve its land preservation mission, The Nature Conservancy requires enormous reserves of liquid cash to acquire real estate. For most land that the Conservancy purchases, monies are advanced to cover expenses as they occur. Funds advanced are paid back through fund raising or through government reimbursement.

The Conservancy's primary financing source for saving land is the LPF which is a long-term capital endowment. The LPF is the Conservancy's own private bank from which funds may be borrowed to purchase natural lands and then repaid; the funds "revolve" as they are returned to the LPF and loaned again to another land preservation project.

Each project is charged an interest rate that is fixed for each fiscal year. This rate is determined by senior management once each fiscal year during the annual budget process. As an incentive to protect the most biologically diverse land, fundraiser projects that have a high biodiversity rating (B4 or B5) are charged 1.5 percent less than the basic rate. The chief financial officer, chief operating officer, and general counsel have the discretion to recommend to the president that the differential rates be applied.

Employee Evaluation

Within The Nature Conservancy, the focus on the mission at hand is applied even at the level of the individual. Each employee is evaluated annually on the basis of two primary criteria. First, the employee is rated with respect to the job description given to the position he or she holds within the company. Second, the employee's performance is evaluated in terms of his or her efforts toward the Conservancy's goals. Through such an evaluation, each employee feels his or her importance and relevance to the mission statement.

The Nature Conservancy utilizes "checks," such as the annual personnel appraisals, to assure that each member of the staff remains committed to and focused on the primary goals set forth in the strategic plan. These processes have two specific goals: (1) to act as a guide for individuals to indicate in which direction to focus their own initiatives, and (2) to encourage an evaluation of their actions before requesting the Conservancy's time or funds.

State Program Performance Ratings

This method of internal feedback has two purposes (1) to provide regional and state directors with the information they need to assist their programs and focus on any problem areas, and (2) To provide an objective consistent measure of progress over time. The rating process is designed to measure the absolute performance of a particular state program without regard to the size or difficulty of operating in a state. Thus, many states may never receive high scores under this system. In the future, a system may be devised to standardize scoring, at which time scoring reports could be released.

Evaluation standards are set as follows:

1st Level: Performance at the very top range of what The Nature Conservancy would hope to have in this program area. Very little room for improvement, outstanding results.

2nd Level: Performance comes close to meeting The Nature Conservancy expectations in this area. Good results, but still significant room for improvement.

3rd Level: Performance is clearly unsatisfactory in this particular area at the present
time.

The standards for measurement are revised annually and include suggestions
from all users.

The categories on which programs are graded follow the goals of the
organization's mission statement. These categories are Identification, Protection
(Projects), Protection (Other), Stewardship, Development (Project/Program),
Development (Operations), Institution Building, State Office Management and
Administration.

The nine major categories are further subdivided into as many as seven
subcategories, and the score in each subcategory is eventually multiplied by 1,
2, or 3 before determining the single rating for the category. The nine major
categories contribute equally to the overall score. To assess a state program,
each of the nine categories should be reviewed separately.

CONCLUSION

The Nature Conservancy's cyclical approach to cost-effectiveness, therefore,
is woven throughout its operational procedures. It does not depend on one or
two specific tools applied periodically to measure cost-effectiveness. Rather, the
methodology is focused on a continuous effort to carry the mission of the
Conservancy throughout all aspects of the organization. By rating and
evaluating each portion of the strategic plan, annual plan, budget, and, finally,
internal feedback mechanisms, cost-effectiveness occurs within each program.

NOTE

1. Each preserve may be composed of a number of land conservation projects
partially owned or protected by conservation easements.

7

Measuring Our Impact: Determining Cost-Effectiveness of Non-Governmental Organization Development Projects

Margaret Bowman, Jorge Baanante,
Thomas Dichter, Steven Londner, and
Peter Reiling, *TechnoServe, Inc.*

INTRODUCTION

Many people in the development field are accustomed to measuring the number of dollars spent, vaccines shipped, loans made, or training hours invested as a sufficient way of estimating the effectiveness of a development project. These factors are signs of progress and can be readily measured. But they do not in themselves reflect development "output." By focusing on efforts, we may lose sight of the true objectives of development work: sustainable results.

But therein lies the question. How can an organization tell if its efforts are creating sustainable beneficial results? How can a "business" with social goals measure the effects of its projects?

TechnoServe keeps its focus on economic and social goals, and monitors its impact in the field, with cost-effectiveness tools. Our cost-effectiveness methods allow us to measure the social or economic impact of our work on beneficiaries' lives and provide a framework for analyzing these changes. The value of our model lies both in its application to enterprise development projects and, more generally, as an approach to analyzing effective results vis à vis invested resources.

WHAT IS COST-EFFECTIVENESS?

We define cost-effectiveness as the ability to achieve project objectives at a reasonable cost. A cost-effective project should yield a return of benefits (to the target group) that is greater than the assisting organization's total investment. In the case of development assistance, these benefits can often be difficult to measure and monitor. They typically involve cultural, social, political, and economic effects. For TechnoServe, this means comparing the costs of running our programs and projects to the positive sustainable impact we have on participant-owned enterprises and their surrounding communities and regions.

Table 7.1
Cost-Effectiveness vs. Benefit-Cost Analysis

Our cost-effectiveness model differs from the conventional benefit-cost analysis in three ways: **(1)** Cost-effectiveness relates to overall financial and *nonfinancial* effectiveness as specified by an organization, whereas benefit-cost methods typically focus only on financial or economic aspects of a project; **(2)** Our cost-effectiveness model analyzes benefits to *project beneficiaries* compared with *our* costs as an assistance organization, whereas benefit-cost methods typically include all costs associated with the project and analyze a project from one perspective, such as that of the government; and **(3)** Benefit-cost analyses usually result in a single number—the larger the better. The results of our method are neither so easy to interpret, nor perhaps so precise. However, the two methods serve different purposes. We geared our analysis to a non-governmental organization's need for a relatively simple, reduced-cost management tool which could be applied to the local economies surrounding development projects.

Fully recognizing the importance of state-of-the-art benefit-cost analysis techniques, several staff members researched benefit-cost and cost-effectiveness processes used by other organizations. We considered the different viewpoints from which the analysis was conducted (country, enterprise/investor, a combination),* the level of accuracy and rigor of the methods, and the useful information which could be learned from the results. After this careful research, we felt that the method we developed would hold external validity. Additional time was spent at the World Bank and at university economics departments discussing debatable issues such as the use of social discount rates (which measure a society's preference for uses on money now vs. later), and simplifying assumptions of financial analysis we proposed to use.

---

*   In economic benefit-cost analysis, the relative value of a project is assessed from a national economic viewpoint and necessarily entails a host of explicit and implicit assumptions about the country's policy preferences. In financial analysis, the relative values are viewed from the perspective of the prospective investor or participant. In TechnoServe's cost-effectiveness analysis, we draw on the techniques commonly used in the above methods, and we further attempt to use measurable indicators consistent with our agency goals and objectives operating in a development program.

Developing a cost-effective project is not the same as developing a project at minimum cost. Containing project costs does not necessarily lead to high project cost-effectiveness, especially if the time frame for analysis is short. For example, a well designed training program may lead to long run gains in program objectives. If cost-containment is our only concern, then valuable effectiveness-enhancing investments in training or other investments with long gestation periods may be foregone because they do not seem to pay off in the short run.

WHY HASN'T COST-EFFECTIVENESS BEEN USED MORE?

Why should development organizations, with their ambitious tasks, bother with cost-effectiveness measures at all? Indeed, to many who feel that the work of development organizations is worthwhile regardless of cost, the idea of evaluating cost-effectiveness is distasteful. In this case, the effort and resources expended are accepted as sufficient proof of a project's value; quantification reduces their worth.

Some do not object to quantifying project evaluation, but they feel that most common tools of measuring cost-effectiveness are inappropriate. Current methods seem more applicable to the for-profit sector, where the primary objective is to maximize return on investment. Making decisions based purely on financial figures does not seem appropriate for nonprofit organizations. With limited knowledge of the methods and the limitations of quantifying complex development objectives, nonprofit organizations have not adopted cost-effectiveness analysis.

Until recently, the worthy and complex goals of development organizations have allowed nonprofit organizations to escape real pressures to prove their effectiveness. We no longer have that luxury. We have new pressures from increasingly better informed donors and shrinking funding pools. To diffuse these pressures, and to advance our profession, we must directly tackle the issue of project cost-effectiveness.

In our experience, well-designed cost-effectiveness analysis is appropriate for most types of development organizations, including nonprofit ones. It is only natural that nonprofit organizations concern themselves with the principles of cost-effectiveness—comparing costs of assistance to end results. We generally have limited funds, rely on donors to support our efforts, and tend to tackle large projects that could use all the resources we can divert to them. By being cost-effective, we can expand our ability to better help more people or add new depth or diversity to our program.

Table 7.2
Cost-Effectiveness Ratio

The Cost-Effectiveness Ratio is calculated from the Financial
Component spreadsheet. It is estimated as follows:

$$\text{Cost-Effectiveness} = \frac{\begin{array}{l}\text{Net Financial Benefits Attributable to TechnoServe Assistance}\end{array} \quad \text{less} \quad \begin{array}{l}\text{Financial Benefits to Group Without TechnoServe Assistance}\end{array}}{\text{TechnoServe's Cost}}$$

The Non-Quantifiable Benefits Rating is a system of weighted values
ascribed to carefully defined:

ECONOMIC BENEFITS
SOCIAL BENEFITS
POLICY BENEFITS

HOW TECHNOSERVE BECAME INTERESTED IN COST-EFFECTIVENESS

TechnoServe's efforts to assess its impact date back to 1975. Our
motivation was an internal one, driven by a desire to help as many people as
possible with our limited resources and to be disciplined stewards of our donors'
money. As a small organization focusing exclusively on enterprise development,
we thought we could easily quantify the benefits of our work and arrive at an
appropriate analog to a corporation's "bottom line" concept of profits as a
measure of success.

Over the next ten years, as we moved from the abstract notion of cost-
effectiveness to attempts to apply a model, we ran into complex issues of
definition. Should indirect costs and benefits be included in the analysis? How
should different levels of infrastructure development and political risk be taken
into consideration when comparing impact between projects or between countries
or regions? We also ran into predictable questions of local currency benefits
versus dollar costs, inflation, and changing rates of interest, as well as headier
issues of unintended consequences, such as how to count the value of work by
other organizations that may have preceded us in a project. We realized that
this exercise involved much more planning and participation by staff than we
had anticipated. In addition, we realized that if we tackled some of these issues,

we would learn more about the nature and impact of our development work. In an effort to control some of these elements, we established some guidelines for the development of the analytical method.

1. *The model needed to be useful enough for our field staff.* Many theoretical issues arose, revealing layers of complexity which could have easily made an already complicated analysis unmanageable. The model needed to be accessible to all of our varied field staff, whatever their professional expertise and academic training. Given these constraints, we consciously kept our method simple for our work in the field.

2. *The model needed to be efficient.* Application of the analysis to our projects could not require staff members to deviate significantly from their existing work. Highly detailed and technical methods, such as those employed by the World Bank on its projects (and about which abundant literature exists), require more information and technical skills than we had easy access to without greatly increasing our expenditures. We had to strike a balance between analytic rigor and expense.

OUR MODEL IN A NUTSHELL

The focus of TechnoServe's work is to transfer managerial, technical, and administrative skills to enterprise owners and members and to help local institutions positioned to assist them. Because our focus is enterprise development, the core of our model includes a measure of enterprise profits (the accepted indicator of business success) and financial returns to project participants. But, because our goals are social as well as economic, we have also developed a means of encompassing other non-quantifiable goals into our project evaluation process.

The resulting system is a combination of two complementary, but distinct, methods of analysis. The first part of the analysis, the *financial component*, calculates a basic *cost-effectiveness ratio* (using relatively standard practices of benefit-cost and net present value analysis). This is derived through an annotated spreadsheet constructed to compare the expected financial gains to those participating in the project to the program cost of providing services. The second part, the *non-quantifiable benefits rating*, is a system of weighted values reflecting other development benefits that cannot be easily translated into dollar amounts.[1]

Each of these components can stand independently to determine project effectiveness. When interpreted together, they present a multidimensional view of our impact and ability to deliver services to the communities in which we work.

THE TECHNOSERVE COST-EFFECTIVENESS MODEL©

In our first attempt to apply cost-effectiveness to our work, we focused too heavily on enterprises as an end in themselves, rather than as a means to an end. As we evaluated the nature of our work, it seemed logical to measure the economic performance of the enterprises we assisted. We had built-in standard criteria: jobs created, wages paid, profits, and so on. In an attempt to identify a relatively objective process employing objective criteria, we used methods commonly applied to corporations and ended up with a rather dry financial analysis of our enterprise assistance.

We found that this was a mistake for a development organization. We assumed that a financially healthy enterprise was sufficient *proxy* for the benefits we hoped would result. (We assumed that through the enterprise, participants would increase their incomes, allowing them to "buy" better health, better housing, and better education.) While not an unreasonable assumption, it remains a matter of speculation unless we track the real long-term effects of our work. After all, an enterprise could be profitable even while the low-income people who participated in it did not make more money. On the other hand, it was possible that an "unprofitable" enterprise could still enable low-income farmers to increase their incomes.[2]

Thus, our early approach focusing on enterprise financial information skipped over the very elements that make our work so important. What we strive to do is improve people's lives, teach them how to work together, transfer technical skills, empower the poor to make their own decisions, and improve national policy toward the poor. The complexity of these elements was hardly captured in the financial records of an enterprise.

As our organization evolved, we did not abandon enterprises as our focus. On the contrary, we strengthened our capability in this regard. What we did do was to explicitly recognize enterprises as the *vehicles* through which we hoped to improve the lives of our beneficiaries, not as ends in themselves. Therefore, to measure our impact and effectiveness we decided to broaden our analysis to include project participants and the immediate community.

Over time, we also became aware of the need to monitor the sustainability of assisted enterprises. We had to find a way to see whether the enterprise was instrumental in producing a *stream of benefits over time* to the people we intended to reach. In the terminology of economics, we were looking for the net value added attributable to our projects. A community derives significantly greater benefits from an enterprise that is successful over fifteen years than from one that fails after two years. If a non-governmental organization is in primary health care, how does it evaluate the effectiveness of a clinic built at low cost that is unused and abandoned or broken down after one year of operation? We needed to address long-term sustainability and its relation to real impact.

Finally, as we learned more about cost-effectiveness, we understood that we would need to keep abreast of traditional literature on benefit-cost analysis, but we also realized that we would have to customize traditional cost-effectiveness methods to our own needs.

MORE DETAILED DESCRIPTION OF THE ANALYSIS

The first step toward developing our method was to evaluate our definition of cost-effectiveness. The criteria we developed grew out of TechnoServe's stated objectives, long-term strategic plans, and the experienced opinions of staff members. The result was a set of working criteria that took into account such factors as:

- Providing ready markets for locally produced goods
- Increasing enterprise profits
- Producing additional jobs or sources of wages for local workers
- Ensuring equitable ownership of enterprise assets
- Ensuring enterprise sustainability
- Increasing participants' sense of control over their lives
- Increasing and sustaining agricultural productivity
- Improving linkages with other areas of the economy
- Affecting national policy
- Being consistent with TechnoServe's skills and resources

Our definitions entailed a broader view of cost-effectiveness than is applied by academics and businesspersons, but we felt that the omission of social, economic, and policy considerations in more traditional methods would not capture our definition of effectiveness. Recognizing that many notable economists have invested significant effort in refining cost-effectiveness analysis techniques, we make an effort to understand and integrate the most widely agreed upon principles of cost-effectiveness into our method.

The Financial (Quantifiable) Component

Conceptually, our model captures all easily identifiable direct financial benefits derived from the enterprise under study and compares them to the amount of money and time TechnoServe must expend to deliver services to

assist it. This information is compiled over time because, while we incur costs
at the beginning of the intervention, the enterprise usually derives increasing
benefits as participants learn to become more self-sufficient.

The financial component of the model focuses on three aspects of the
participants' projected income which constitute our definition of financial return
to beneficiaries: (1) increased community-level (farmers, suppliers, owners)
incomes, including on-farm consumption; (2) increased enterprise profits (before
dividend payments, mandated reserves, reinvestment, or taxes); and (3)
increased aggregate salaries, wages, and benefits to enterprise employees or
directly contracted services. Each must be calculated as a net incremental return
(i.e., the difference between the return attributable to the project and the return
that would have occurred in the absence of the project). This calculation results
in what economists call net value added.   Projections are made for two
scenarios: with TechnoServe assistance and without it.   These figures are
projected out ten years beyond the termination of intensive TechnoServe
assistance to the project.[3]

We feed data for each project into a cost-effectiveness financial spread-sheet
appropriate to that project type (see Figure 7.1).   To keep the financial
measurement consistent and "in check," only direct benefits to project
participants are included. By restricting our financial analysis to direct and
measurable returns, we produce lower, more conservative benefit estimates.

In our model, financial benefits are more difficult to calculate than are
costs. Standard methods for estimating financial and economic returns are rigid
and complex, and they include such concepts as shadow pricing, foreign
exchange components, and taxes which will probably not affect the management
decisions of small enterprises. We chose to trade off precision for simplicity.
Our analysis is limited to estimating only the financial benefits (value added) to
the owners of the projects. We do not attempt to estimate the broader benefits
that accrue to the economy as a whole.

For example, the salary and wage component of financial returns in our
model pertains to funds injected into the local economy from new project
employment. In rural areas, we assume that any new local jobs created by the
project are drawing *new* people into the wage-earning labor force, and thus
represent new production. We judge whether it is worth our effort to estimate
the opportunity cost of a farmer's time (and include it in the analysis) when he
may not have had previous steady employment or was not remunerated for his
work. When the value of the farmer's time is easily measured, we do estimate
and include it in calculations. Such simplifications could be disputed, but we
feel the development of a vibrant rural economy is often more valuable (in terms
of stimulating the local economy, avoiding urban immigration, etc.) than is the
contribution of salaries and wages, and we feel satisfied that we have considered
the trade-offs of making this simplifying assumption.

Figure 7.1
Quantifiable Benefits Analysis Worksheet

PROJECT: Preston Cooperative Oil Palm Farmers Society COUNTRY: Ghana DATE: January 1991 BASE YEAR FOR C/E ANALYSIS: 1990

CATEGORIES Subcategories	1985	1986	1987	1988	1989	1990 (BASE YEAR)	1991	1992	1993	1994	1995	1996	1997	1998	1999	2000
I. BASIC PARAMETERS:																
Exchange Rate Used (local currency/dollar)	50.00	145.00	180.00	280.00	340.00	345.00										
Annual Inflation Factor						37.00%										
US Treasury Bill Rate	7.49%	5.97%	5.83%	6.00%	6.40%											
II. ECONOMIC BENEFITS:																
A. Benefits Without TechnoServe's Assistance:																
1. Farmer & Processor Income	0	0	0	0	1051333	1345042	2210000	2525250	2651513	2784088	2623293	3069457	3222990	3384077	3553280	3730944
2. Enterprise Income	0	0	0	0	0	0	0	0	0	0	0	0	0	0	0	0
3. Salaries and Wages Paid	0	0	0	0	2548800	3426500	5499000	5773950	6062648	6365780	6684069	7018272	7369186	7737645	8124527	8330754
B. Benefits With TechnoServe's Assistance:																
1. Farmer & Processor Income	0	0	0	0	16502851	19731160	29483833	30960125	32508131	34133538	33840215	37632225	39513837	41489529	43564005	54742205
2. Enterprise Income	0	0	0	0	-169748	-151924	120873	126840	133182	139841	146833	154175	161884	169978	178477	187400
3. Salaries and Wages Paid	0	0	0	0	4211964	5513712	8524506	8901506	9297356	9712999	10149423	10607669	11088827	11594043	12124520	12681521
C. Incremental Benefits of TechnoServe Assistance:																
1. Farmer & Processor Income	0	0	0	0	15471518	18386118	27273833	28434875	29856619	31349450	31916922	34562768	36290907	38105452	40010725	42011261
2. Enterprise Income	0	0	0	0	-169748	-151924	120873	126840	133182	139841	146833	154175	161884	169978	178477	187400
3. Salaries and Wages Paid	0	0	0	0	1663164	2087212	3025506	3127556	3234709	3347219	3465354	3589397	3719641	3856398	3999993	4150767
D. Present Value of Incremental Benefits																
1. PV of LC Past Benefits (1984-1990)	0	0	0	0	18661427	58747129										
2. PV of LC Future Benefits (1991-2000/SDR=10%)						223786401										
3. Present Value of Incremental Benefits (US$)						$818,998										
III. COST OF TECHNOSERVE ASSISTANCE:																
1. TechnoServe "01-21" Cost (a)	0	0	0	37,611	67,646	64,500	12,500	3,000	0	0	0	0	0	0	0	0
2. TechnoServe Fee Income (b)	0	0	0	360	1,074	957	375	0	0	0	0	0	0	0	0	0
3. Annual Net TechnoServe Cost (a-b)	0	0	0	34,251	66,572	33,543	12,125	3,000	0	0	0	0	0	0	0	0
4. Compound Net TechnoServe Cost prior to 1991	0	0	0	37,251	106,059	146,390										
5. NPV of Net TechnoServe Cost after 1990						14,046										
6. Present Value of Net TechnoServe Cost						$160,435										

IV. TECHNOSERVE'S COST-EFFECTIVENESS RATIO ===== $818,998 DIVIDED BY: $160,435 EQUALS 5.10

Table 7.3
Definitions of Cost-Effectiveness Terms

Net Income to Farmers: The actual and/or expected income to farmers net of their enterprise-related farm-level production costs (this varies by project type). Income to farmers within the target population is calculated net of what they earned previous to TechnoServe assistance. Net increases in on-farm consumption are also added.

Net Enterprise Income: Increased enterprise income is the most direct financial benefit of enterprise assistance. Net enterprise income is calculated before taxes, dividends distributed, etc. It its drawn from projections or actual data from the enterprise income statement, depending on when the analysis occurs.

Salaries and Wages Paid: These consist of salaries and wages paid by the enterprise to its staff. Other workers' wages may be appropriate to include, such as those who interact regularly with the enterprise, and local people whose incomes have risen due to increased volume of activity.

Benefits without TechnoServe Assistance: Any financial returns in the form of farm-level income, enterprise profits, and salary and wages that exist prior to TechnoServe assistance are calculated in baseline studies. We assume these benefits would continue if TechnoServe had not become involved. Also included here are other factors which would have increased benefits even with out TechnoServe's assistance.

Total Financial Benefits: Sum of the first three items above, minus the fourth, calculated in local currency (so information is useful at field level).

Total Financial Benefits in 1988 Currency: Total financial benefits above are converted to current units for the year of analysis (e.g., 1988) using the Consumer Price Indices for each country. this allows us to account for the effects of past inflation.

Present Value of Financial Benefits in Local Currency: Stream of financial benefits is revalued in the year of analysis (1988) to account for the opportunity cost of money in each country. Benefits in the past are worth more; benefits in the future are discounted according to the social discount rate assumed for the country. (The Social Discount Rate estimates the opportunity cost of money to society, which may differ considerable from a discount rate derived purely financially. Generally, the social discount rate varies from 8.5% to 12.5% according to the strength of the economy. TechnoServe assumed this rate to be 10% for this exercise.)

TechnoServe's Costs: We include all costs directly associated with the project, including administrative costs in the field and attributable support costs of the main office. These costs are largely incurred in local currency and require no conversion. Costs incurred in dollars are converted to local currency.

Net Present Value of Financial Costs: TechnoServe's net financial costs are discounted using the same Social Discount Rate used to discount the benefits in the numerator.

Table 7.3 (continued)

> **Fee Income:** this is subtracted from TechnoServe's costs, because it represents payment from the participant groups for services. From TechnoServe's perspective, the project is more effective if the participants pay fees because such payments reinforce commitment and encourage businesslike behavior. Fees are generally minimal relative to the total technical assistance costs and are determined by the beneficiaries' ability to pay. While fee income is not intended for our cost recovery, it must still be accounted for in the in the spreadsheet because it directly offsets TechnoServe costs to the project. Since these fees reduce net enterprise income, they are added back into the numerator.

The second financial returns component looks at the bottom line of the enterprise itself. Net enterprise profits are an obvious gain to beneficiaries since they are the enterprise owners. Also, any increases in enterprise net assets/net worth are clearly a benefit to the owners. Taxes paid are a cost to the enterprise, but from TechnoServe's perspective, taxes paid are a benefit to the local and national economies (they add to the legitimacy of the enterprise), and thus are included in our calculation.

These total net financial benefits constitute the value added by the project. They are brought to a present value in the year of analysis using standard techniques for handling inflation and other discounting/compounding factors. We then compare project benefits to an analogous present value representing TechnoServe's costs.

The cost-effectiveness ratio (C-E ratio) equals the present value of the project's net benefits divided by the present value of its costs. Notice in the equations below that our model views financial benefits from the project participants' view-point, whereas costs are viewed as TechnoServe's. This is an important element of the model because it reflects our view of development assistance. We do not want to measure how TechnoServe benefits from our development assistance, but rather how our beneficiaries benefit. By mixing the perspectives of the financial analysis when measuring the effectiveness of our organization, we depart from traditional benefit-cost analysis to focus our development objectives on the low-income people we assist.

Also, TechnoServe's costs may constitute only a modest portion of the total development assistance injected into a community or region. Therefore, we look at the total net financial returns we feel are most directly attributable to TechnoServe's participation in the activity and compare it to our costs. If we effectively use TechnoServe's development investment to leverage other significant investments in a project, such as new roads, electrical service, debt financing and the like, so much the better. Our resources are being put to good

Table 7.4
Cost-Effectiveness Ratio

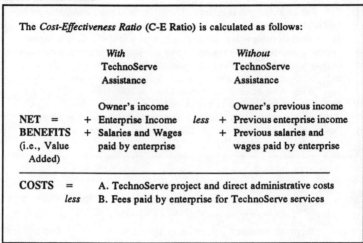

The *Cost-Effectiveness Ratio* (C-E Ratio) is calculated as follows:

		With TechnoServe Assistance		*Without* TechnoServe Assistance
NET = BENEFITS (i.e., Value Added)	+ +	Owner's income Enterprise Income Salaries and Wages paid by enterprise	*less*	Owner's previous income + Previous enterprise income + Previous salaries and wages paid by enterprise
COSTS = *less*		A. TechnoServe project and direct administrative costs B. Fees paid by enterprise for TechnoServe services		

use. Again, it is a matter of perspective: we are looking for the best use of our limited resources, and the best return to beneficiaries on our own investment.

The cost-effectiveness ratio summary sheet is an abbreviated version of a set of spreadsheets completed by TechnoServe field staff. (See Figure 7.1 for a sample). Each summary item, such as "owner income," is calculated from a supporting spreadsheet using actual figures and projections.[4] See Figure 7.1 for a spreadsheet estimating benefits. For example, when working with agricultural enterprises, we derive farmer income from crop yields, input prices, crop prices, labor costs, and other costs of production. The enterprise income calculation, much like a business plan, includes production variables, input prices, administrative expenses, packaging costs, depreciation, and interest.

This analysis, therefore, requires that estimates, and preferably actual financial details of the enterprise, be collected regularly. The more accurate the data are, the more useful the calculations will be. The analysis also requires accurate, up-to-date records of how much is spent on each project and associated administrative costs. However, even with tentative pre-project estimates of costs and benefits, this tool is useful for identifying unrealistic expectations of development projects.

The analysis proceeds as follows:

- Past financial returns, calculated in local currency, are converted to current values using annual Consumer Price Indices for each country, and then added. (This accounts for local inflation.)

- To obtain a current discounted value, future returns are discounted by a country's discount rate to account for the opportunity cost of money invested for social purposes. (See Table 7.3 for details on Present Value of Financial Benefits in Local Currency).

Assistance costs have two components: (1) costs incurred in local currency in the country where the project is carried out and (2) costs incurred in U.S. dollars in our home office or elsewhere. Costs incurred in U.S. dollars are converted to local currency using the same exchange rate that TechnoServe receives when it converts dollars. The local currency costs plus the dollar costs converted to local currency are added together to give us total costs. These are the total costs that go into the denominator of our C-E ratio.

- Past/future costs are compounded/discounted by the same discount rate used to discount the benefits in the numerator (i.e., the social discount rate applicable in the country). The use of this rate makes the impact of discounting costs comparable to that of discounting benefits. More important, by carrying out the analysis entirely in local currency and discounting with the social discount rate, we are maintaining the analysis within the context of the economy in which the project is operating. It could be argued that the opportunity cost of the U.S. dollars used by TechnoServe is better reflected by a discount rate drawn from the U.S. economy. We make the assumption that the resources are committed to the country independent of the choice of which project they will support. Therefore, it is the local opportunity cost of capital which is most relevant.

The cost-effectiveness ratio is calculated by dividing the present value of benefits by the present value of associated costs. For example, a ratio of 1:1 tells us that the financial benefits expected to be derived by the project participants are equal to the financial costs incurred by TechnoServe, and a ratio of 5:1 suggests that the financial benefits are five times as great as our expenditures. This ratio, and its supporting spreadsheets, provides us with information about our financial bottom line, the analog to business profits that we were searching for.

The Non-Quantifiable Component

The financial component tells only part of the story. We realize that failing to look at the non-quantifiable benefits can distort the reality of a project, both positively and negatively. To address the remaining criteria in our definition of a cost-effective project, we developed a second component of our methodology, the non-quantifiable benefits rating sheet (NQBR).

We developed a list of non-quantifiable benefits, divided into three categories: social, economic, and policy benefits. Because TechnoServe has

Figure 7.2
NQBR Sheet

TECHNOSERVE, INC.
COST EFFECTIVENESS ANALYSIS
Non-Quantifiable Benefits Summary Worksheet

PROJECT: Prestea cooperative oil palm farmers society   COUNTRY: Ghana   DATE: January 1991

	Weight	Samuel Danso Project Advisor Value	Weighted Value	Esther Adjetey Project Advisor Value	Weighted Value	Paul Warmka Country Director Value	Weighted Value	Average Scores for all Raters
I. SOCIAL BENEFITS:								
A: Improved Managerial & Technical Skills	5	14	70	14	70	16	80	73
B: Increased Access to Public Services	4	12	48	11	44	10	40	44
(e.g., banking, extension, health)								
C: Increased Control over Quality of Life	3	14	42	12	36	12	36	38
D: Greater Participation for Marginal Groups	2	12	24	12	24	16	32	27
(e.g., women, minorities)								
E: Increased Community Solidarity	1	11	11	11	11	12	12	11
Category Totals:	15		13.0		12.3		13.3	12.9
II. ECONOMIC BENEFITS:								
A: Increased and Sustainable Productivity	5	16	80	15	75	13	65	73
B: Enterprise Replicability	4	17	68	11	44	15	60	57
C: Increased Enterprise Sustainability	2	15	45	13	39	12	36	40
D: Increased Employment	2	15	30	15	30	13	26	29
E: Improved Backward/Forward Linkages	1	15	15	15	15	15	15	15
Category Totals:	15		15.9		13.5		13.5	14.3
III. POLICY BENEFITS:								
A: Improved National Policy Environment	5	10	50	10	50	13	65	55
for Rural Enterprises								
B: Regional/Commodity Sector Policy Impact	5	11	55	10	50	19	95	67
C: Institutional Policy Impact	5	14	70	13	65	12	60	65
Category Totals:	15		11.7		11.0		14.7	12.4
Total, All Categories	45		596		542		607	582
Non-Quantifiable Benefits Indicators			13.3		12.0		13.5	12.9

RATINGS GUIDELINES:
* VALUE = 5-9   : Project has actually had a negative effect with respect to this benefit.
* VALUE = 10   : Project has had neither a positive nor a negative effect in this benefit category.
* VALUE = 11-20   : Project has had a positive effect with respect to this benefit category.

overarching goals affecting each country program, we established standard sub-categories within the three headings for the entire organization. Examples of social benefits include "increased access to public services" and "greater participation for marginalized groups." Economic benefits include "increased employment" and "improved backward/forward linkages." Finally, policy benefits include "improved national policy environment for rural enterprises" and "institutional policy impact." (See Figure 7.2 for a sample NQBR sheet.)

Evaluations equally divide rated "weights" among social, economic, and policy benefits. This reflects our organizational aims of extending benefits through targeting the beneficiaries we originally intended to assist, keeping national/regional economic goals in mind, and having a policy impact. However, we determine the relative importance of each sub-category through discussions with staff to bring the categories in line with the strategic goals of

Figure 7.3
TechnoServe Cost-Effectiveness Methodology

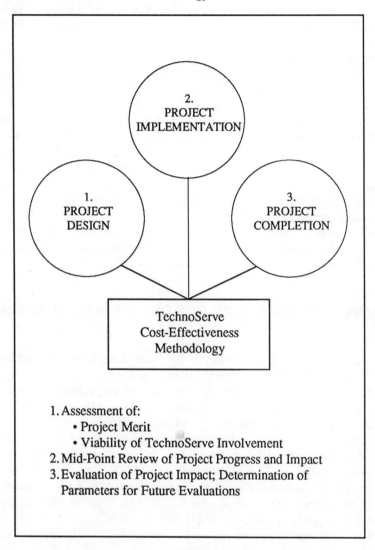

each country and program. These sub-headings remain stable until any major shifts in program focus necessitate changes.

Once the NQBR sheet weights are complete for each country, the individual projects are rated independently by five persons. To keep a balanced perspective of non-quantifiable benefits, designated TechnoServe field staff, including the project manager and the country program director, evaluate the project. These staff members are responsible for the project and have the knowledge and experience to assign a value representing the degree to which TechnoServe's intervention had an impact (positive or negative) on the given category.

Two additional evaluators rate the project. One is a project participant who is involved as an owner or other kind of direct beneficiary. We believe the opinions of those who are to be served by the project are very important to include. The other is an independent observer who has no vested interest in the project; that is, the observer neither a TechnoServe employee nor a project beneficiary. It should, however, be someone very knowledgeable about the project. For example, it could be an extension agent or loan officer who has known the ownership group well and has followed its progress closely.

The five ratings are averaged, and comments or discrepancies among them are noted in the final rating sheet. Later these sheets are used to instigate important discussions among project advisors. The averaged rating sheet, at a glance, identifies the non-financial benefits of pursuing the project. Furthermore, the comments accompanying each rating provide information about which aspects of the TechnoServe intervention had an impact on the given category.[5]

EXAMPLES OF THE APPLICATION OF COST-EFFECTIVENESS ANALYSIS

Technoserve's Cost-Effectiveness (C-E)© methodology was designed for use at three points in a project's development (see Figure 7.3). At the project design stage, the analysis provides an assessment of the project's merits and the viability of TechnoServe involvement. Baseline data provide some actual figures for the analysis, but most measurable elements are projections.

As the project develops, we apply the analysis for midpoint review of project progress and impact. Initial projections may be updated to reflect actual figures, and revised projections of the future can be made. At this stage, the C-E ratio and the NQBR sheet will be much more useful for feeding back information to project managers. There is still time to reflect on progress and address any issues that the analysis points to. Depending on the project and the enthusiasm of local staff for using the cost-effectiveness tool, such analysis during implementation may be conducted annually.

Ex post analyses of projects that have "graduated" from TechnoServe assistance served as complements to our evaluation processes. Because TechnoServe usually maintains monitoring contracts and friendly relations with groups beyond our original period of assistance (and because our field staff are nationals, so they are still in the area), we have the opportunity to collect data about the projects after assistance has ended. By looking at the analyses conducted over the life of the project, and by comparing them with analyses of similar projects, we can learn a lot about how to make our approach more cost-effective. Furthermore, analysis at project completion helps to determine parameters for future evaluations.

HOW TO INTERPRET AND USE SUMMARY SHEETS

The cost-effectiveness analysis was intended to yield results that inform a manager of a project's progress and effectiveness in a summary form. Each analysis requires that spreadsheets and various NQBR sheets be carefully constructed by the field advisors. However, the final presentation of the analysis to other TechnoServe staff and managers is in the form of summary sheets. A completed analysis includes (1) a short description of the project and an explanation of the major cost-effectiveness findings; (2) a financial component summary spreadsheet; and (3) an averaged NQBR.

Summary sheets tell a great deal about a project's effectiveness. First, the project description sets a context in which the results should be analyzed. It might include information about currency devaluations, inflation, the extent to which civil unrest impacts the project area, the nature of the assistance TechnoServe is providing, and consideration of the beneficiary group.

Second, the C-E ratio summary sheet clearly specifies the benefits and other key indicators that are useful for project monitoring and evaluation. The breakdown of actual and projected benefits to farmer income, enterprise income, and salaries and wages allows the interpreter to determine from where the real returns of the project were derived. Major variations in trends can be quickly identified. This sheet can then serve as a tool for identifying problem areas of the enterprise's finances that can be further explained by project managers.

Comparing C-E ratio sheets completed at different points in a project's development is illuminating because actual figures do not always match expectations. Through readjustments of projections, staff improve their ability to gauge their expectations of the financial returns from an enterprise. The summary ratio at the bottom of the spreadsheet indicates the cost-effectiveness of the project, but alone, without a breakdown of the variables, it does not convey the nature of the benefits provided. Third, the NQBR sheet details the benefits that accrue to the project participants. Field staff who perform the ratings fill in accompanying comments on the values they assign to communicate the nature of changes in benefits. We established ranges for rating values so that a rating of 1 indicates neither a positive nor a negative effect on the benefit category. Therefore, values significantly lower or higher than 1 (0.5 or 2 are the extremes) indicate notable effects on non-quantifiable benefits. A low NQBR (under 1) tarnishes a high C-E ratio when these two components are interpreted together to determine project cost-effectiveness. Such a case might

Table 7.5
Sample Summary Results from Cost-Effectiveness Field Tests

The following is a representative sample of the cost-effectiveness results from some of TechnoServe's community-owned, agriculturally related enterprises.

COUNTRY & PROJECT	PROJECT TYPE	C-E RATIO	NQBR
SALVADOR 1	Livestock management and rice production project	3.46:1	1.74
SALVADOR 2	Tomato processing plant	1.06:1	1.60
COSTA RICA 1	Fruit marketing co-op	9.28:1	1.41
COSTA RICA 2	Food and farm supplies co-op	6.00:1	1.40
PERU 1	Vegetable, fruit & cattle co-op	1.68:1	1.45
PERU 2	Regional water management	29.5:1	1.65
PANAMA 1	Multiservice consumers co-op	8.20:1	1.27
PANAMA 2	Agricultural products marketing and consumer retail store	9.59:1	1.34
ZAIRE 1	Production and marketing of cassava, maize, and ginger & charcoal production business	0.62:1	1.47
ZAIRE 2	Agriculture production	0.91:1	1.42
KENYA 1	Cultured milk processing business	1.86:1	1.49
KENYA 2	Community-owned water utility	4.94:1	1.47
SUDAN 1	Small farmer credit program	13.61:1	1.45
GHANA 1	Oil palm milling business	0.71:1	1.50

imply that the enterprise achieved financial gains at the expense or exclusion of social or policy benefits. Consistently low NQBR could then alert TechnoServe staff to redirect their efforts toward social and policy benefits.

Interpreted together with the C-E ratio summary sheet, NQBR do not vary as much from project to project as C-E ratios do. This consistency is probably a result of careful project and beneficiary selection at the outset of our assistance. Meaningful comparisons can be made between NQBRs calculated in earlier years and those calculated in later years for the same project. Initially, the rating indicates what non-quantifiable benefits are expected, and as the project proceeds, later ratings reflect progress made.

Also, if the analysis is conducted for all projects in a region of a given country, we can compare projects sectorially to determine barriers to growth at the policy level. Such barriers could include government restrictions, our own management capabilities, lack of human resources, lack of infrastructure, and so on.

The comparative value of our cost-effectiveness analysis does have an important limitation. Comparisons are only valid in relative terms. If two projects in different countries both have C-E ratios of 5, for example, we can say that they both generate benefits five times greater than costs. We cannot say they both produce $5 of benefits for $1 of cost! This is because the analysis is carried out in local currency. This was a conscious trade-off we made. Our initial methodology, which required conversion of local currency values to dollars, had the unfavorable impact of permitting distorted exchange rates to skew the results. A project in one country may look very poor compared to one in another country simply because of an overvalued rate of exchange. By using local currency we avoid this problem and make comparisons possible in relative terms. Absolute comparisons require a careful application of the exchange rate to the factors in the C-E ratio.

Analysis of the cost-effectiveness results will lead us to consider many possibilities so that we can improve our programs by confronting these problems. At the very least, this analysis allows us to recognize the economic and social challenges before us so that we may introduce a healthy mix of projects into our overall portfolio. The summary results shown in Table 7.5 the box are characteristic of the cost-effectiveness analysis as applied to a sampling of current and past TechnoServe projects. The C-E ratios can vary from 0 to any positive number. We hope that our projects will result in *at least as many* positive financial benefits as the cost we invest as a development organization, and so we are pleased with ratios of 1 to 1 (1:1) or greater. Our project analyses have yielded results varying from 0.05:1 to 50:1. The wide range of results reflects the diversity of project conditions in which TechnoServe works.

COST-EFFECTIVENESS APPLIED TO TECHNOSERVE PROJECTS

In the sample of our results (see Table 7.5), the majority of C-E ratios are favorable, and the non-quantifiable rating results were all favorable. This level of summarizing the cost-effectiveness results, however, cannot indicate why the results turned out as they did. In fact, all of these cases were calculated when we were still converting costs and benefits to U.S. dollars, and these results are no doubt influenced by distortions in relative exchange rates. Summary numbers, such as those presented here, only give a general indication of whether the overall benefits a project returns to beneficiaries exceed the costs to TechnoServe.

Although we designed the C-E ratio to be the financial bottom line of the enterprise, this must be interpreted along with the NQBR to determine whether the project is cost-effective. Take the example of a project that turns out to be the only source of employment. Furthermore, the women have learned valuable skills in group organizing which have carried over into other aspects of their lives, and two women have learned bookkeeping (resulting in an NQBR of 1.7). The cost-effectiveness result of such a project, therefore, is strongly influenced by our interpretation of the value of non-quantifiable benefits. In this case, we feel the benefits outweigh the costs, but we must then consider whether enterprise development is the most efficient way to achieve these objectives.

We constantly think about the trade-offs that we must often make in development projects. The cost-effectiveness method makes these trade-offs more clear and helps us to consciously decide how far we are willing to go to promote monetary benefits to beneficiaries at the "expense" of other benefits, or vice versa. These are not easy decisions, but we have to make them every day. In the end, our evaluation of project effectiveness comes from further interpretation of the cost-effectiveness analysis and from discussions with the project participants and managers.

ANALYSIS OF THE METHOD

TechnoServe has invested considerable effort in designing and refining its cost-effectiveness method. We feel that it meets our expectations of a management tool that can relate benefits and costs to objectives. It is easy enough for our program staff to understand and use, feeds back necessary project information to program staff, and has imposed more discipline on our staff in that they must consider both the quantifiable and the non-quantifiable benefits of our work. In the course of our efforts, we came to appreciate the value of the cost-effectiveness measurement *process* itself. Some TechnoServe employees concluded that the process was ultimately more important than its eventual product. Through structuring the analysis, debating the elements, and assessing the impact that variables have on the end result, our staff learned more about the implications and impact of their projects than the C-E results reflect.

For the first time, we have an effective and comprehensible tool that accurately represents the project process. The method forces us to be explicit about our assumptions and expectations for project performance and impact. Done properly, the quantitative element starts with the enterprise business plan, and, building upon it, matures into a more sophisticated model of expected impact appropriate for sensitivity analysis. Discussions of the non-quantifiable aspects of the model help focus staff attention and interest on the underlying developmental objectives of our work and more clearly illuminate our overall objectives in day-to-day project decision making. As we improve our understanding of cost-effectiveness results, they will play an increasing role in strategic planning, monitoring, and evaluation.

The implementation of the cost-effectiveness process has strengthened

TechnoServe's already considerable commitment to the responsible stewardship of limited donated resources and the maintenance of a broad development perspective on our work. The C-E model also provided the impetus for a substantial revamping of our internal project-related management information system. We found that while we had collected the information we need to complete the cost-effectiveness calculations, we had not done so consistently or in a form that was easy to manipulate. We examined the efficiency of our current reporting systems, debated the usefulness of aggregated data at different levels of our organization, and developed parameters for collecting, storing, and comparing financial and socioeconomic data for an organizationwide database.

Another important aspect of the cost-effectiveness model is its use in fund raising. Cost-effectiveness analysis allows us to respond more authoritatively to donor/funding agency concerns that might arise regarding the impact and use of donated resources. In addition, because we feel the analysis reflects the complex nature of enterprise development, this tool educates as well as informs donors. For example, in the current debate about credit versus nonfinancial assistance to enterprise projects, a common assumption is that nonfinancial assistance costs too much. A cost-effectiveness analysis of these approaches (focusing on impact) applied to similar projects over a reasonable time frame may dispel some of these assumptions and move the debate such questions as "Under what conditions is one approach more cost-effective?" or "What mix of services is most effective for what circumstances?" If we can build sustainable projects with a demonstrated positive impact, and if we can communicate the notion that a strong enterprise can continue to deliver a stream of benefits over time, then donors may commit to more long-term project funding.

Despite the positive aspects of developing a cost-effectiveness methodology, we realize its limitations. It would be nice to produce results that can easily be interpreted as good or bad. However, our method does not produce such clear-cut results, and we therefore rely on educated users of the information to correctly interpret how cost-effective the project is/was. Several project variables can influence high or low ratings. These include the timing of the analysis, legislated restrictions on wage rates, and other development activities that complement or restrict the enterprise, government policies, and natural disasters, among others.

Still, TechnoServe feels ready to address our effectiveness even though we cannot predict what the outcome and the implications of this analysis might be. Cost-effectiveness allows for relative comparisons. It is not an ordinal determination of an individual project's or program's success or failure. We recognize the danger that others might misuse our methods to make uninformed, cut-and-dried analyses of complex events. We do not intend to judge projects solely on the basis of cost-effectiveness results. Other monitoring and evaluation tools, particularly the sound and experienced judgment of our field staff, will never be replaced by a cost-effectiveness formula.

WHY IS COST-EFFECTIVENESS APPROPRIATE FOR NGOs?

Development-oriented non-governmental organizations (NGOs) should regularly evaluate and assess the effects of different project approaches. NGOs need to examine some of the methods of achieving different development goals in order to identify those that are cost-effective. With this information in hand, we can move ahead as a profession to "scale up" our impact and effectiveness. In this way, cost-effectiveness analysis is an important step toward improving overall NGO development impact.

Project sustainability and impact are now key determinants of development effectiveness. NGOs need to show that the results of our projects are achieving stated goal, and that the results are sustainable over a reasonable period of time. As development organizations, we need to focus on meaningful outputs.

NGOs are also stewards of donors' money. As such, we have a responsibility to spend funds wisely. Cost-effectiveness methods can make clear what our programmatic objectives are, how we have achieved them, and what the cost is. The analysis imposes a discipline on organizations so that they can compare the ultimate impact of their work to their costs. Some large donors are already establishing norms and encouraging others to impose more rigorous and measurable standards for their work.

LESSONS LEARNED

In the course of developing our cost-effectiveness methodology, we learned several lessons:

- *Pursuing organizational cost-effectiveness requires strong commitment by top management.* Initially, the process is time-consuming and requires substantial internal coordination; it might not have developed without the backing of our president and Management Committee.

- *The process of assessing cost-effectiveness can be as important as evaluating the results.* Creating a cost-effectiveness process forces us to be explicit about assumptions and expectations for project performance and impact. Moreover, it provides an ideal opportunity for staff training in long-term developmental objectives and motivates staff members to think more broadly and concretely about the social, economic, and policy consequences of their efforts.

- *Reliable cost-effectiveness calculations are impossible without sound historical data (including baseline financial and socioeconomic measurements) and an ability to make reasonable projections into the future.* The former comes with a comprehensive evaluation and reporting system. The latter requires sound financial skills as well as an in-depth understanding of the operating environment, including likely policy developments, economic trends, and so on.

- *Since not all projects are alike, special effort must be taken to design a flexible, yet consistent cost-effectiveness model.*

- *The results of cost-effectiveness analyses should not be taken out of context.* All results must be understood within the environment in which they were generated—the national political climate, macroeconomic conditions, program's stage-of-growth, and so on. We have a responsibility to present figures clearly and in context. Users of our cost-effectiveness methodology must be careful not to make false comparisons between results drawn from widely different industries, sectors, countries, or regions.

- *Each country appears to have its own range of acceptable cost-effectiveness numbers.* A considerable number of projects must be evaluated to determine those ranges before the end result has any inherent meaning.

- *We opted to carry out the analysis in local currency because a straight conversion of local currency to U.S. dollars does not accurately capture the full extent of benefits, nor does it allow for comparisons between countries.* We continue to seek ways to factor currency imbalances into our model. One method we are exploring is a purchasing power parity index such as that used by the International Comparison Project (ICP).[6]

- *Cost-effectiveness results must be handled with care and should be used by management as one input among many for making strategic decisions.*

- *While highly useful in the assessment of our direct enterprise development activities, the TechnoServe cost-effectiveness methodology is not appropriate for the analysis of institution-building efforts.* To capture the cost-effectiveness of this work, we need to modify our current model.

- Use of a cost-effectiveness formula could pressure us toward easier projects. A project is cheaper, for example, if participants are better educated or if assistance is provided in a city. For example, in a city, transportation costs will be lower and the chances of a project's success will be generally higher due to better infrastructure. *Measures should be taken to remind field staff that higher numbers in the quantitative components of the formula are not necessarily better.* These numbers will be tempered by lower marks in "reaching marginalized groups, increased community solidarity, etc." if projects do not reach TechnoServe target clients in target areas.

IS COST-EFFECTIVENESS FOR EVERYONE?

There is great diversity within the NGO community. Different development sectors are addressed by different NGOs. Within the same sector, NGOs may use different approaches, use different kinds of staff, or have different levels of resources.   And within a single organization, there may be significant differences in types of projects. No individual measure can ever tell the entire story of a program's or an organization's effectiveness.

Because of this diversity, and because there are few industry norms in development, it is especially important that NGOs wishing to measure cost-effectiveness take the general literature on the issue with a grain of salt. No single cost-effectiveness "system" or formula is likely to be applicable or adaptable to every type of organization. However, programs with enterprise and credit components should be expected to undergo quantification and are primary candidates for cost-effectiveness analysis. After all, our reasons for pursuing enterprise and credit projects are that they increase incomes and jobs, enliven economies, and increase economic participation of the poor—all of which are measurable goals.

The purpose of conducting cost-effectiveness exercises is not to reduce development efforts to a number; the real aims are to be more explicit about goals, planning, and monitoring and to learn to interpret the information to improve project management. These are appropriate exercises for many types of projects.

We acknowledge that the model we present may not be appropriate for other development activities in the exact form presented, but the principles underlying cost-effectiveness seem to be useful for most programs and projects. There is little question that such an analysis triggers important questions within an organization that would otherwise probably not be raised. It seems that the discipline generated in the organization by the cost-effectiveness process has positive reverberations in all aspects of our work, especially strategic planning. We hope that the lessons extracted from TechnoServe's experience with cost-effectiveness analysis can be adapted to other organizations' needs.

NOTES

1. See Editor's Note in note 5.

2. Some enterprises, by law, cannot earn a profit. However, through rebates to members, access to services, reduced input prices, or higher prices negotiated for goods sold, members/owners of the enterprise can increase their incomes.

3. We adopted the convention of projecting accrued project benefits for a period of ten years following TechnoServe assistance—an average period of existence we expect for the enterprises we work with. We considered the average expected life of healthy enterprises, the unstable country surroundings, and our realistic expectation that the enterprises, will continue to exist after our assistance had ended. In particular cases, a different duration for the benefit stream may be appropriate; (e.g., forestry projects) however, after ten years, these benefits (when discounted) are negligible. Similarly, we adopted the convention of ignoring the residual (liquidation) value of a project's assets. But, again, in certain cases, such as a capital-intensive irrigation system scheduled for a major rehabilitation in its eighth year, this convention may be contravened.

4. Since not all projects are alike, special effort must be made to design spreadsheet

templates that address the elements of C-E ratio summary sheet that are suitable for each project type and the assistance TechnoServe is providing (e.g., production, agro-processing, service cooperatives, marketing).

5. Editor's Note: At the time of the writing of this chapter, a lively debate is under way at TechnoServe regarding the NQBR. We have sought the opinion of highly respected authorities who have advised us against using an aggregate, weighted index to assess the non-quantifiable benefits. The most serious questions about our NQBR were raised by Price Gittinger, William Ward, and Peter Kilby, all of whom have publications cited in the references to Chapter 1. The conclusion that one reaches based on their observations is that weighting and aggregating factors as we have done could disguise critically important factors int he project evaluation process (both ex ante and ex post).

Two alternatives emerge from these observations. First, the quantitative analysis could be expanded to take into account some of the non-quantifiables. This is the approach preferred by Kilby, who refers to the methodology explained in his *Searching for Benefits*. Gittinger and Ward, on the other hand, suggest that in-depth research would have to be done on non-quantifiable impacts before the factors and their appropriate weights could be identified. They find our current factors to be somewhat arbitrary and unsubstantiated by empirical evidence. In the absence of such research they recommend a simple listing and scoring of the non-quantifiable factors. The scoring system explained above could be used, but the scores would not be weighted or aggregated. This would force review of each of the factors individually and lead to a closer examination of very positive or very negative factors that would get lost if they were aggregated. If, for example, the project has a very favorable impact on women, it may justify accepting a lower cost-effectiveness ratio. The high score on this factor might be lost if it were aggregated with all other factors.

6. The real value of benefits in the financial component of the model does not accurately represent the value of purchasing power in each country. This tends to undervalue the stream of benefits that we attribute to each project and prevents us from making realistic comparisons of benefits between countries. To capture this notion, we have experimented with the ICP indices as conversion factors. If the ICP were factored into the conventional exchange rate, the stream of benefits (in local currency) might increase by as much as ten (El Salvador) or 20 (Kenya) times.

REFERENCES

Brown, Maxwell L. *Farm Budgets: From Farm Income Analysis to Agricultural Project Analysis*. Baltimore: Johns Hopkins University Press, 1979.

Gittinger, Price J. *Economic Analysis of Agricultural Projects*. Baltimore: Johns Hopkins Press, 1982.

Jenkins, Glenn P., and Arnold Harberger. *Cost-Benefit Analysis of Investment Decisions*. Cambridge, Mass.: Harvard University Press, 1986.

Kilby, Peter, and David D'Zmura. *Searching for Benefits*. Special Evaluation Study no. 28. Washington, D.C.: Agency for International Development, 1985.

Mishan, Edward J. *Cost-Benefit Analysis: An Informal Introduction*. London: George Allen and Unwin, 1982.

Ray, Anandarup. *Cost-Benefit Analysis: Issues and Methodologies*. Baltimore: Johns Hopkins University Press, 1984.

Roemer, Michael, and Joseph J. Stern. *The Appraisal of Development Projects: A Practical Guide to Project Analysis with Case Studies and Solutions*. Westport, Conn.: Praeger Publishers, 1975.

Sassone, Peter G., and William A. Schaffer. *Cost-Benefit Analysis: A Handbook*. San Diego: Academic Press, 1978.

Squire, Lyn, and Herman G. Van der Tak. *Economic Analysis of Projects*. Baltimore: Johns Hopkins University Press, 1975.

8

Evaluating the Cost-Effectiveness of Housing and Human Service Providers

Debbie Cohen Pine, *Pine and Associates*

INTRODUCTION

More and more donors, managers, and trustees of nonprofit organizations are striving to develop appropriate ways to evaluate the cost-effectiveness of housing and human service providers. Unlike businesses whose performance can be measured by the "bottom line," nonprofits have broad social goals that are extremely difficult to quantify.

This chapter describes the methods that Shelter Network of San Mateo County (California) created to evaluate the cost-effectiveness of two of its transitional housing programs for the homeless. It describes the process used to answer such questions as:

- How can we assess the impact of our programs on people's lives? How can we measure actual outcomes, as opposed to program inputs?

- How can we quantify the benefits of providing a roof over a homeless person's head or of raising someone's sense of self-esteem?

- How can we develop a common scale to measure disparate human needs? (For example, we generally think of food, money, education, and emotional support in terms of different units of measurement.)

- How can we leverage our limited resources to assist even more homeless people more effectively? How can we judge the value of adding incremental services (e.g., job placement assistance) to existing programs?

- How can we conduct a cost-effectiveness evaluation without making the staff feel threatened?

This chapter does not attempt to present a step-by-step primer on how to conduct a cost-effectiveness evaluation. Instead, it summarizes how Shelter Network successfully developed "hard measures for soft services." Hopefully, it will inspire others facing the challenges of quantifying "fuzzy" benefits of nonprofit service providers. Like Shelter Network, other nonprofits conducting cost-effectiveness evaluations are likely to find that the increased understanding gained through this introspective process is far more valuable than the specific numerical results.

This chapter begins with a description of the crisis of homelessness in San Mateo County, California, and an overview of Shelter Network. A discussion of Shelter Network's motivations for participating in this evaluation and an explanation of the methodology and results follow. The chapter ends with a description of the organizational impact of the evaluation and of the lessons learned.

FACES OF THE HOMELESS

Fewer than 300 beds exist nightly for San Mateo County's 8,000 to 10,000 homeless residents.[1] The county's 2,000 government-subsidized housing units have zero vacancy rates, with waiting lists that have been closed for many years.

Shelter Network's Executive Director Christina Sutherland explains: "Homeless people are individuals whose traits, ages, occupations, and histories mirror those of the general population. The faces of the homeless in San Mateo County reflect a cross-section of low-income America: working people who have only recently fallen through the 'safety net' due to a convergence of primarily economic factors."[2] Most are long-time county residents who are homeless for the first time. More than half are high school graduates.[3]

Over 30 percent of the county's homeless are employed, but earn too little to meet their basic human needs.[4] Executive Director Sutherland adds: "What was the working poor is now the working homeless. In the past ten years, 66 percent of the County's new jobs have paid minimum wage, which is less than the $10,000 annual rent for the average two-bedroom apartment."[5] With county housing costs among the highest in the nation, most of those earning low and moderate wages cannot bridge even a short-term interruption of income. Lacking a strong support system, a single emergency—such as a layoff, chronic or sudden illness, absence of medical insurance, substance abuse, divorce, or eviction—can create homelessness.

SHELTER NETWORK'S RESPONSE TO THE CRISIS

Shelter Network's core mission is to help homeless residents of the county regain stability through transitional housing programs with supportive social services. As described in an organizational profile, "Shelter Network provides county-wide coordination of comprehensive homeless services aimed to reintegrate the homeless back into community life and empower them towards independent lives...Our traditional housing programs seek to arrest the cycle of homelessness, re-linking families and individuals with stable incomes, jobs and permanent housing."[6]

Unlike emergency shelter programs that solely provide a roof over someone's head, Shelter Network's philosophy is that stop-gap measures are insufficient.   Therefore, Shelter Network's programs offer participants a comprehensive and coordinated approach by providing

- Counseling, crisis intervention, and case management

- Job development and housing search assistance

- Workshops on employment, self-sufficiency, nutrition, housing rights, and other topics

- Personal financial an budgeting assistance

- Food, clothing, furniture, and household items

- Support groups

- Advocacy

In addition, through information and referral, Shelter Network functions as a critical entry point to an even broader network of services.

Formed in 1987, Shelter Network sponsors transitional housing facilities through four distinct programs.   This evaluation focused on two of these programs: Family Crossroads, which assists families; and Turning Point, which assists single adults.   Both Family Crossroads and Turning Point offer a nurturing, resourceful environment that helps clients confront crises, stabilize, and overcome the causes of their homelessness.   While in the programs, participants must conduct a job search if unemployed; seek permanent housing and save money toward the first month's rent of their next home.   Participants also meet regularly with their case managers and attend weekly workshops and support groups, discussing topics relevant to homelessness, such as self-esteem and self-sufficiency.

Family Crossroads

The Family Crossroads complex of nine one-bedroom apartments accommodates families for an average stay of two to three months.   In 1988, Shelter Network initiated follow-up case management for Family Crossroads. This service helps families who have graduated from the program to maintain steady incomes and avoid recurring homelessness.   Monthly family support group meetings and twice monthly home visits by a case worker provide encouragement, social service support, and referrals.

From its inception in 1988 through the time of this evaluation in 1991,

Figure 8.1
The Pyramid Model

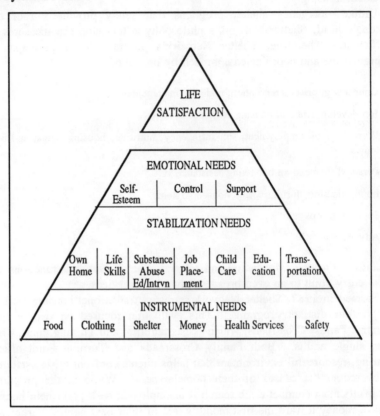

Family Crossroads had provided transitional housing for over 150 homeless families, or more than 500 parents and children. Over 50 percent of the parents successfully obtained employment while participating in the program. Seventy percent of the families regained permanent housing within an average of eight weeks of program participation.

Turning Point

Homeless single adults constitute one-third of San Mateo's homeless residents, yet are the population least served by community housing assistance and public welfare programs. For example, almost all one-night motel vouchers are reserved for families. Until Turning Point opened, no year-round facilities existed for homeless singles. Turning Point fills this crucial service gap, forming a bridge between homelessness and self-sufficiency.

Turning Point maintains a facility that can house thirty nine residents in semi-private rooms. Participants stay an average of three to six months. Turning Point participants have generally been homeless longer than the newly homeless participants in Family Crossroads. Compared to the parents in Family Crossroads, fewer Turning Point participants are employed full-time. Unlike Family Crossroads, Turning Point has no formal follow-up program. From its inception in 1989 through 1991, Turning Point had served more than 200 adults, over half of whom obtained steady incomes and permanent housing.

MOTIVATION FOR EVALUATION

Since the organization's inception, Shelter Network management has been seeking better ways to measure program efficacy and to quantify qualitative outcomes. In addition, management has always been eager to stretch its limited resources to assist even more homeless people and to provide greater program depth and diversity.

In the spring of 1991, one of the organization's major donors, The Peninsula Community Foundation, invited Shelter Network to help develop methods for evaluating the cost-effectiveness of nonprofit organizations. The specific challenge was either (1) to evaluate Shelter Network's programs using TechnoServe's model for evaluating the cost-effectiveness of non-governmental organization development projects or (2) to create a more appropriate model for evaluating the cost-effectiveness of housing and human service providers and to develop baseline data.

Shelter Network quickly accepted this invitation and began work by forming an evaluation team comprised of staff and a program officer of the Foundation. The author of this chapter served as an outside consultant and managed this project.

METHODOLOGY

Design

The evaluation team first considered using existing models to quantify the value and efficiency of Shelter Network's programs. At its first meeting, the team agreed that merely quantifying intangible outcomes—such as getting an individual off the streets and into permanent housing—was enough of a challenge without valuing every outcome in dollar terms, as is the norm with cost-benefit analysis. Time and resource constraints further ruled out cost-benefit analysis. In addition, TechnoServe's cost-effectiveness ration was inappropriate for our evaluation because all of the desired outcomes of Shelter Network's programs (except for participants' incomes and savings) were nonfinancial.

Since neither cost-benefit models nor TechnoServe's cost-effectiveness model was applicable to Shelter Network, the evaluation team decided to develop a new methodology. Like TechnoServe, we defined *cost-effectiveness* as the ability to achieve desired outcomes at a reasonable cost. Our methodology compared program costs from the perspective of the organization offering assistance to program benefits from the perspective of participants. While this approach is common to most cost-effectiveness models, it differs from cost-benefit models, which typically analyze all benefits and costs from a single perspective.

Our goal was to evaluate the cost-effectiveness of Shelter Network in a way that would

● Strike an appropriate balance between analytical rigor and time/expense

● Provide practical tools that staff could utilize independently in the future

● Assist management in decision making

● Provide baseline results that Shelter Network can use to track changes in program cost-effectiveness over time

Description

Desired Program Outcomes: The Pyramid Model of Human Needs

Perhaps the greatest challenge for the evaluation team was defining and measuring the benefits of Shelter Network's programs. We achieved this by analyzing Family Crossroads and Turning Point within a framework based on Maslow's hierarchy of human needs. Our Pyramid Model, shown in Figure 8.1, represents the needs addressed by Shelter Network. The basic concept behind the hierarchy of needs is that until people's most basic needs are met, their higher-level needs are less likely to be satisfied. For example, a person who lacks food and shelter is less likely to feel a high sense of self-esteem or to feel in control of his or her life. The Pyramid Model identifies four levels of needs: instrumental needs, stabilization needs, emotional needs, and the need for life satisfaction.

The foundation of the pyramid is comprised of *instrumental needs* for

● Food

- Clothing

- Shelter

- Money

- Health Services

- Safety

The second level from the bottom of the pyramid is comprised of *stabilization needs* for

- Job Placement

- Substance Abuse Education and Intervention

- A Home of Ones' Own

- Child Care

- Education

- Transportation

- Life Skills (e.g. job development, budgeting, parenting skills, health or legal information)

Continuing up the pyramid, the third highest level is comprised of *emotional needs* for feelings of

- Self-Esteem

- Control

- Support

The pyramid's highest level is *life satisfaction*, (i.e., reaching one's full potential and enjoying the highest quality of life. Maslow calls this "self-actualization." Although Shelter Network believes its programs help participants develop more satisfying lives, enabling homeless people to attain life satisfaction is beyond the scope of a three-month transitional housing program.[7]

Based on this framework, we defined *individual needs* (i.e., food, clothing, education, self-esteem, etc.) as the "building blocks" of the pyramid. We defined *human needs* as the combined instrumental, stabilization, and emotional needs shown in the Pyramid Model. We then defined the desired outcome of Shelter Network's programs as increasing the degree to which participants' *human needs* are met over time (which we referred to as increasing participants' level of satisfaction of human needs.)

From Shelter Network's perspective, some individual needs have a higher priority than others.   Therefore, we also assigned specific weights to each individual need shown in the Pyramid Model.[8]

Timeframe of Analysis

Our model measured the degree to which program participants' *human needs* were met at various points in time:

- *Time 1*: The day before a program participant enters transitional housing
- *Time 2*: The day before the participant leaves transitional housing
- *Time 3*: Three months after the participant leaves transitional housing

We then compared program costs to program outcomes for the year ending May 1991.

Ratings to Characterize the Meeting of Human Minds

The evaluation team developed a five-point scale to characterize the degree to which each *instrumental* and *stabilization need* was satisfied at Times 1, 2, and 3. This scale assigned ratings as follows:

Rating	Explanation
1	Required service; no service was provided
2	Required service; the need was **minimally** met
3	Required service; the need was **moderately** met
4	Required service; the need was **intensively** met
5	Did not require service

However, we thought participants would have great difficulty using the above scale to characterize the level of satisfaction of emotional needs at any given point in time. For example, we thought participants would have difficulty characterizing their level of self-esteem three months after program completion. Therefore, we developed a different five-point scale to rate *emotional needs* over time. In other words, the second scale rated self-esteem, control, and support on a relative basis, as opposed to an absolute basis.

We assigned the following ratings to characterize the change in the level of satisfaction of each *emotional need* over time:

Rating	Explanation
-2	*significant decrease* in the degree to which the need was met
-1	*Some decrease* in the degree to which the need was met
0	*No change* in the degree to which the need was met
1	*Some improvement* in the degree to which the need was met
2	*Significant improvement* in the degree to which the need was met

Implementation

Measuring Costs

Program cost per participant served as the numerator in the cost-effectiveness ratio described below. For each program, we calculated the overall cost per participant, as well as the amount spent per participant to address each of the individual needs.

Shelter Network had solid figures for the total costs of Family Crossroads and Turning Point. However, we had difficulty identifying the specific costs required to address each individual need, such as safety or *emotional support*. To do this, we estimated the percentage of staff time spent addressing each individual need, and, where possible allocated all additional "hard dollars" spent, e.g., for bus tickets, food, or job placement. We fully allocated all overhead to Shelter Network's programs because the programs could not exist without financial management, fund raising, and other core administrative services.

Measuring Outcomes

By comparing the levels of satisfaction of participants' human needs three months after program completion and before program intervention, we assessed the net outcomes, or benefits, of Shelter Network's programs.[9] We obtained the majority of the outcome data from a special oral survey conducted by case workers of twenty-six people who participated in the programs in the year ending in May 1991.[10] In addition, we obtained data from standard intake, exit, and follow-up forms, as well as from case worker progress notes.

Appendix A presents sample questions from the survey of Family Crossroads graduates. Appendix B describes how we used the survey data to calculate the overall program benefits—the aggregate change in the level of satisfaction of human needs over time. This figure served as the denominator in the cost-effectiveness ratio described below.

Calculating Cost-Effectiveness

By comparing the program cost to the net benefits to program participants, we calculated cost-effectiveness using the following ratio:

$$\frac{\text{Program Cost}}{\text{Weighted Change in the Satisfaction of } \textit{Human Needs}}$$

We used this formula to calculate the overall cost-effectiveness of Turning Point and Family Crossroads, as well as the cost-effectiveness of each program's services that address each of the individual needs. For example, for Turning Point, the program cost for food was $27,172. The weighted change in satisfaction of participants' human needs was 812. Therefore, the cost-effectiveness of food services at Turning Point was

$$\frac{\$27,172}{812} = \$33.46$$

Using this formula, more cost-effective programs and services will attain lower cost-effectiveness ratios.

In addition to using the ratio described above, the evaluation team examined the following additional indicators of cost-effectiveness:

- Program cost per participant
- Change in the satisfaction of human needs per participant
- Change in the satisfaction of human needs per $1 cost

The latter indicator is simply the inverse of our cost-effectiveness ratio.

Results

We obtained the results shown in Appendix C for Turning Point for the year ending in May 1991. The overall cost-effectiveness ratios were 7.31 for Turning Point and 9.07 for Family Crossroads. At this point, we cannot judge whether Family Crossroads and Turning Point achieved the desired outcomes in a cost-effective manner because we have no standards for comparison.

However, we obtained the primary result that we were seeking for this initial cost-effectiveness analysis, which was to obtain valuable baseline data that Shelter Network can use as bench marks in setting cost-effectiveness goals for the future. Shelter Network can periodically repeat this evaluation and track changes in the cost-effectiveness ratios over time. Such longitudinal analysis can produce significant insights. For example, if Family Crossroads established on-site child care services, Shelter Network could assess the incremental value of these services by comparing next year's cost-effectiveness ratio for child care with this year's baseline value. By comparing cost-effectiveness ratios before and after such program modifications, management can assess whether programs can (1) achieve comparable outcomes with lower costs or (2) significantly improve outcomes by spending marginally more in certain areas.

In judging these results, it is important to remember that cost-effectiveness ratios are impacted by a number of outside factors. For example, the cost-effectiveness ratios of Family Crossroads and Turning Point are affected by the health of the overall economy and by the rate at which outside agencies refer participants to Shelter Network's programs.

The evaluation team initially intended to make cross-program comparisons of the cost-effectiveness ratios of Turning Point and Family Crossroads. However, we soon realized that differences in the nature and number of program participants would nullify such comparisons. Because Turning Point serves single adults, as opposed to families, it serves more participants and, therefore, has a lower per-participant cost.[11] These differences in scale and capacity utilization explain much of the discrepancy between the cost-effectiveness ratios of the two programs.

Limitations

Our methodology has a number of limitations, including the following:

- Results of this cost-effectiveness analysis are far less precise than are results of cost-benefit analysis. We cannot immediately interpret isolated cost-effectiveness ratios as "good" or "bad," as we can with cost-benefit ratios. Instead, we must interpret changes in program-specific cost-effectiveness ratios over time or make cross-program comparisons.

- Comparing cost-effectiveness ratios of different programs is only valid when the programs have approximately the same scales and goals. Family Crossroads and Turning Point both provide transitional housing with supportive services for the homeless of San Mateo County. Yet comparisons of their cost-effectiveness ratios are not very meaningful because one program serves families, whereas the other serves single adults. Because low-income-housing providers have substantially different philosophies and goals, developing an industrywide model of cost-effectiveness is extremely difficult.

- Management should never cut a program solely on the basis of its cost-effectiveness ratio. Instead, management should judge the cost-effectiveness ratio as part of a comprehensive program evaluation that considers additional factors, such as funding availability and alignment with organizational goals.

ORGANIZATIONAL IMPACT

This cost-effectiveness methodology enhanced Shelter Network's ability to analyze performance, demonstrate program effectiveness, and promote more efficient use of resources. For the first time ever, Shelter Network tracked the per-person cost of providing services to address individual needs. The process imposed more rigorous and measurable standards on Shelter Network. It discouraged attempts to judge program impact by counting inputs and focused management on results and outcomes relative to costs. This cost-effectiveness evaluation has improved Shelter Network's ability to respond to funders who voice concerns about the impact of their donations.

Conducting this analysis helped the organization articulate program objectives, clarify assumptions, and focus attention on trade-offs. The evaluation process fosters improved planning and monitoring and encourages "big picture" thinking. As a result of this analysis, Shelter Network plans to redesign its internal data collection systems so that its standard intake, exit, and follow-up forms routinely gather more of the information required for this cost-effectiveness evaluation. Structuring the analysis, debating the elements, and gathering data educated staff about program impacts. This process has begun to build staff capabilities for ongoing self-evaluation.

Staff Reaction to the Evaluation

The evaluation team encouraged participation of staff who could provide required information, as well as staff whose buying into the process was critical to the success of this effort. The executive director and the director of programs and services were members of the evaluation team. Others involved in this effort included the director of administration and finance, who provided cost data, and case workers, who surveyed program graduates.

While staff members were genuinely interested in assessing the success of Shelter Networks's services, the evaluation team initially faced some staff skepticism. A few staff members indicated that, regardless of its cost, Turning Point had a moral obligation to continue operations since it filled a critical service gap for homeless single adults. Some staff members voiced concerns about what might happen if we found that one of Shelter Network's programs was far more cost-effective than the other or that neither program was particularly cost-effective relative to programs of other housing providers.

These concerns diminished when staff understood that the results of this initial cost-effectiveness analysis would primarily provide baseline data. In addition, management's enthusiasm for this evaluation helped build staff support. Overall, staff members were quite willing to help and eager to learn the results of this analysis.

HOW COST-EFFECTIVE IS ANALYZING COST-EFFECTIVENESS?

Shelter Network's executive director initially asked, "Should Shelter Network commit resources to this type of rigorous statistical analysis, when the greatest pressure is to commit resources to ongoing program operation?" Yes. All nonprofit organizations should evaluate the efficiency and effectiveness of their programs. The key question is: What type and level of evaluation are appropriate?

The art of conducting a cost-effectiveness evaluation is to strike a balance between analytical rigor and limited time, resources, and information. Shelter Network's experience demonstrates that nonprofit organizations can develop practical methods to evaluate programs with services that are extremely difficult to quantify.

Nonprofit organizations will be more inclined to make serious commitments to analyzing cost-effectiveness if donors will fund such evaluations or tolerate higher overhead in organizations conducting internal evaluations. Shelter Network's experience demonstrates that cost-effectiveness analysis improves stewardship of donated funds. This type of evaluation is worth the cost to nonprofits if it fosters organizational introspection. In the end, the process of cost-effectiveness analysis is as valuable to the organization as the final product is.

APPENDIX A: Sample Questions from the Survey of Family Crossroads Program Graduates

The survey of Family Crossroads program graduates included questions such as the following:

- Before you came to Family Crossroads, was your child care situation
  ___ Not adequate___ Adequate___ More than adequate
  ___ Did not need child care

- Before you came to Family Crossroads, was any community agency providing your family with child care services?
  ___ Yes   ___ No

- Compared to while you were living at Family Crossroads, how much support do you feel you have now from friends, family, and/or community agencies?
  ___ Very much more___ A little bit more___ The same
  ___ Less   ___ Much less

APPENDIX B: Methodology for Assigning Ratings from the Family
Crossroads Survey Data

We assigned a rating of 1 (required service; no service was provided) if a
respondent's answers to the first two survey questions shown in Appendix A
indicated, first, that before she came to Family Crossroads, her child care need
was not adequately met and, second, that no community agency was providing
her family with child care services. On the other hand, we assigned a rating of
4 (required service; the need was intensively met) if she answered, first, that
before she came to Family Crossroads, her child care need was more than
adequately met, and second, that a community agency was providing her family
with child care services. If she did not need child care, we assigned a rating of
5 (did not require service).

Furthermore, we assigned a rating of -1 (some decrease in the degree to
which the need was met) if the respondent answered that compared to when she
was living at Family Crossroads, she now had less support from friends, family,
and/or community agencies.[12] Below is a sample completed rating form for a
recent immigrant.

We calculated an average weighted rating for the degree of satisfaction of
each individual need for Turning Point participants at Times 1, 2, and 3, as
listed below. (To avoid skewing the data, we treated participants who did not
require service for a particular individual need, such as Substance Abuse
Education and Intervention, as a separate group.) Next, we quantified the
degree to which program participation impacted the meeting of each individual
need by subtracting the average weighted Time 1 rating from the average
weighted Time 3 rating. Finally, we summed these values for the individual
needs to calculate overall program impact (i.e., the weighted change in the level
of satisfaction of participants' human needs over time).

Table 8.1
Calculation of the Weighted Sum of Time 1 Ratings for Turning Point Participants

Stabilization Needs	(A) Sum of T1 Ratings of Sample Participants Needing Service	(B) Weighting Factor	(C) = A * B Weighted Sum of T1 Ratings of Sample Participants Needing Service	(D) Number of Sample Participants Needing Service	(E) - C/D Avg. Weighted T1 Rating for Sample Participants	(F) Total Number of Program Participants	(G) = E * F Aggregate Weighted Sum of T1 Ratings
Job Placement	22	3.0	66.1	13	5.1	172	874.5
Drug/Alcohol Ed.	14	3.0	42.1	7	6.0	172	1,033.5
One's Own Home	14	51.5	721.0	14	51.5	172	8,858.4
Education	36	3.0	108.2	14	7.7	172	1,328.8
Transportation	27	3.0	81.1	12	6.8	172	1,162.7
Life Skills	15	3.0	66.1	14	3.2	172	553.6
Child Care	N/A						

Completed Rating Form for a Recent Immigrant

	Time 1	Time 2	Time 3
Instrumental Needs			
Food	2	3	5
Clothing	3	3	3
Shelter	1	2	3
Money	1	2	2
Health Services	3	3	3
Safety	1	2	2
Stabilization Needs			
Job Placement	1	2	1
Substance Abuse Ed. and Int.	5	5	5
Own Home	1	1	5
Education	1	3	3
Transportation	1	2	3
Life Skills	1	2	3
Child Care	5	5	5

	Time 2 vs. Time 1	Time 3 vs. Time 2
Emotional Needs		
Self-Esteem	2	2
Control	1	2
Support	2	-1

Table 8.2
Cost-Effectiveness Results for Turning Point

Human Needs	(A) Program Cost	(B) Aggregate Weighted Change in Satisfaction of Human Needs	(C) = A/B Cost-Effectiveness Ratio: Program Cost per Change in Satisfaction of Human Needs	(D) Number of Program Participants	(E) = A/D Program Cost per Participant	(F) = B/D Change in Satisfaction of Human Needs per Participant	(G) = B/A Change in Satisfaction of Human Needs per $1 Cost
Instrumental Needs							
Food	27,172	812	33.46	172	157.98	4.72	0.03
Clothing	7,490	849	8.82	172	43.55	4.94	0.11
Shelter	85,577	1,070	79.95	172	497.54	6.22	0.01
Money	14,319	332	43.10	172	83.25	1.93	0.02
Health Services	14,726	554	26.60	172	85.62	3.22	0.04
Safety	4,700	1,218	3.86	172	27.33	7.08	0.26
Stabilization Needs							
Job Placement	26,069	517	50.45	172	151.56	3.00	0.02
Drub/Alcohol Ed.	11,224	591	19.01	172	65.26	3.43	0.05
One's Own Home	29,694	27,841	1.07	172	172.64	161.86	0.94
Child Care	NA	NA	NA	NA	NA	NA	NA
Education	12,964	443	29.27	172	75.37	2.58	0.03
Transportion	7,847	301	26.03	172	45.62	1.75	0.04
Life Skills	12,642	997	12.69	172	73.5	5.79	0.08
Emotional Needs							
Self-Esteem	19,645	2,278	8.62	172	114.22	13.24	0.12
Control	19,645	2,278	8.87	172	114.22	12.88	0.11
Support	19,645	2,278	8.87	172	114.22	12.88	0.11
Overall	313,359	42,869	7.31	172	1,821.85	249.21	0.14

APPENDIX C: Cost-Effectiveness Results for Turning Point

For both Turning Point and Family Crossroads, the cost-effectiveness ratio for obtaining one's own home was far lower than the cost-effectiveness ratio for any other individual need. This is because obtaining one's own home is the predominant focus of Shelter Network's programs. This one individual need received a weight of approximately 50 percent. Furthermore, the level of satisfaction for obtaining one's own home improved substantially when Crossroads participants obtained permanent housing after leaving the programs.

These initial results indicated that both Turning Point and Family Crossroads were particularly cost-effective in meeting participants' emotional needs, presumably, in large part through meetings with support groups and case workers.   Despite high costs, the high cost-effectiveness ratios for Job Placement in both programs rekindled management discussions of redistributing caseloads to enable one staff member to focus more concentrated effort on this area.   In conclusion, although these initial results are enlightening, Shelter Network management could derive more accurate cost-effectiveness ratios for each individual need in the future by conducting a staff-time allocation study to more accurately assess staff time spent addressing each individual need.

NOTES

1. Hunger and Homeless Action Coalition. "Living in the Shadow of Affluence," June 1990.

2. Christina Sutherland, Executive Director of Shelter Network.   Interview, February 26, 1992.

3. Shelter Network of San Mateo County statistical data, May 1991.

4. Hunger and Homelessness Action Coalition.   "Living in the Shadow of Affluence," June 1990.

5. Christina Sutherland, Executive Director of Shelter Network.   Interview, February 26, 1992.

6. Shelter Network of San Mateo County collateral information, 1990.

7. To keep the methodology simple, and stay within available time and resource constraints, the Pyramid Model only quantified benefits to program participants. A more comprehensive cost-effectiveness analysis could also include benefits to society at large, such as increased employment, productivity, and savings; decreased number of people living in the streets, jails, and psychiatric wards of hospitals; reduced crime; increased tourism; increased community solidarity; and improved knowledge of patenting skills.

8. We assigned a total weight of 100 to each program. For Family Crossroads, we assigned a weight of 50 to one's own home, assigned a weight of 5 to each of the three emotional needs, and allocated a weight of 35 equally across the remaining twelve individual needs. Child care received zero weight for Turning Point participants since the program explicitly excludes children. Therefore, we rescaled all other Turning Point

weights proportionally.

9. This corresponds to calculating the net change in the satisfaction of participants' human needs from Time 1 (before program intervention) to Time 3 (three months after leaving transitional housing). To obtain additional insight about when changes in the satisfaction of participants' human needs occurred, we also compared the level of satisfaction of human needs at Time 1 vs. Time 2 (while living in transitional housing), and at Time 2 vs. Time 3.

10. Approximately half of the respondents had participated in Family Crossroads, and approximately half had participated in Turning Point. Conducting a random sample of a population that contained a significant number of homeless people would have cause us to exceed our available time and resources. Therefore, the evaluation team derived a broadly representative sample that we believe provides a reliable cross-section of the population of program participants.

11. Capacity utilization was much higher at Turning Point that at Family Crossroads. With semi-private rooms, Turning Point quickly fills every vacancy with another single adult. Family Crossroads, on the other hand, has units designed to hold families of five. However, Family Crossroads' units are not always fully occupied because family size has little bearing on which families are admitted to the program.

12. An issue arose regarding how to isolate outcomes that we could fairly attribute to Shelter Network's programs. Shelter Network provides some services directly to participants. Through information and referral, Shelter Network also links participants to and even broader network of services. The evaluation team felt it was appropriate for collaboration and coordination with other service providers to increase Shelter Network's cost-effectiveness. Therefore, our cost-effectiveness ratio includes effects of assistance obtained—but not of costs borne—by other services providers.

9

Improving Management Decisions in Primary Health Care: Relating Costs to Improvements in Coverage

Lynne Miller Franco, *University Research Corporation/Center for Human Services*

INTRODUCTION: COST-EFFECTIVENESS ANALYSIS IN HEALTH CARE

Cost-effectiveness analysis (CEA) is a method for evaluating or comparing positive and negative consequences of *alternative* uses of resources.[1] It should not be confused with the evaluation of costs and effectiveness of a single option. CEA has traditionally been used to compare how much effect can be achieved for a fixed budgetary input or, conversely, how much input would be required to achieve a fixed level of effect. This type of analysis was developed to assist policy makers in deciding among a fixed number of alternatives. Over the last twenty years, CEA has been applied in health care contexts domestically and internationally to evaluate new methods for prevention, diagnosis, and treatment[2] and to compare various combinations of service interventions.[3]

In its most traditional health care applications, CEA has focused on measuring resource inputs and health outcomes (e.g., lives saved, births averted). CEA has generally been applied as a planning and evaluation technique to compare options that did not produce similar products, such as nutrition services and curative services. The dissimilarity between types of health services restricted analysts to evaluating effects using broad health status measures, such as deaths averted.

The traditional CEA often requires extensive data collection and analysis to produce reliable outcome measures. Collection and analysis of cost data are also time-consuming. As a result, many cost-effectiveness analyses have not examined the "production" process in detail and, thus have contained many inherent assumptions about the relationship between costs and health service activities and between these activities and outcomes.

THE PAHOU PRIMARY HEALTH CARE PROJECT AND "COST-EFFECTIVENESS" ANALYSIS

We wish to propose another type of "cost-effectiveness" analysis, better suited to ongoing management: cost-coverage analysis. This cost-coverage framework can be applied to evaluate and compare strategies for achieving coverage during the planning and evaluation phases of a project or program, but it is also useful for making strategic adjustments in resource utilization during project implementation.

This cost-coverage framework was developed by the Pahou Primary Health Care (PHC) Project staff in order to analyze and develop feasible, low cost strategies for achieving high levels of coverage with PHC interventions. The cost-coverage analysis provided project staff with data for comparing strategies for achieving coverage and with estimated costs for making these strategy changes, as well as helping them to examine the equity of the community financing system in subsidizing preventive care for the poorer groups. Although the examples in this chapter will come exclusively from the rural developing-country setting, the same framework is easily adaptable for other health care settings.

The Pahou PHC Project, initiated in 1982, is a national demonstration pilot project for management of PHC in Benin, West Africa. Although the project has received external funding,[4] it is basically a Beninese effort. The project was created to address the question, How can PHC services be designed and implemented so that they are sustainable and effective? The project serves a population of 17,000, and while the project area is divided "administratively" into fifteen villages, the population lives in more than sixty hamlets. Services include maternal care, growth monitoring for children, immunizations, and curative care. The project catchment area was initially divided into three zones, each implementing a different service delivery model:

●   Zone A: In this centralized model, preventive and curative services are provided at a health center on a daily basis by two nurses, a midwife, and several health aides.

●   Zone B: Preventive and curative services are delivered by village health workers in a village health hut or during home visits. Monthly growth monitoring and immunization sessions are conducted in every hamlet by a nurse. Supervision is monthly.

●   Zone C: Preventive and curative services are delivered by village health workers in their homes or during home visits. Growth monitoring and immunization sessions are conducted every six weeks in the major villages. Supervision visits are made every six weeks.

Figure 9.1
The Health Care System

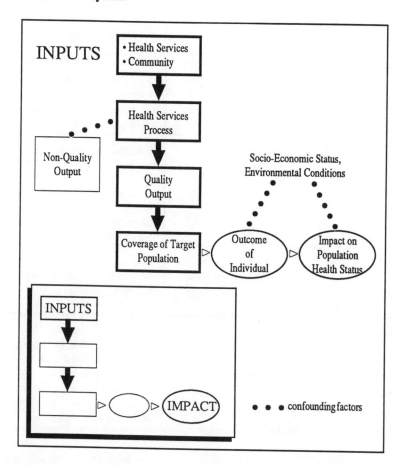

THE COST-COVERAGE ALTERNATIVE TO COST-EFFECTIVENESS ANALYSIS

The value of the cost-coverage framework developed in the Pahou PHC Project comes from its capacity to help managers focus on changes or improvements in their programs: how they could measure them and how they are using their resources to achieve these changes. The cost-coverage framework provides a model for monitoring coverage and its most important determinants and for evaluating the level of effort (resources) used to address these determinants. Managers, using a cost-coverage analysis, can better understand what goes on in the "black box" of health services production.

Table 9.1
Determinants of Effective Coverage: Deviations and Indicators
(Pahou PHC Project for Childhood Immunizations)

COVERAGE DETERMINANT	DEFINITION	COVERAGE INDICATOR
AVAILABILITY	transforming the given structure into service capacity	% of children having reached their first birthday for whom all vaccines are available at the health center
ACCESSIBILITY	transforming spacial distribution of service capacity into one that can be reached by the population	% of children having reached their first birthday for whom quarterly immunization sessions have been given at less than two kilometers from their home before their first birthday
UTILIZATION	producing contact with the target population	% of children having reached their first birthday who have received at least one immunization
EFFECTIVE COVERAGE	transforming contact into effective service coverage -- quantity and quality	% of children having reached their first birthday who have received 3 DPT, 3 Polio, and 1 Measles immunization during the period, and when the cold chain was functioning

The cost-coverage framework differs in scope from traditional CEA. Figure 9.1 shows the health system, with resources coming from multiple sources. These resources, or *inputs*, are transformed through health service *processes* into *outputs* (services delivered). These services, received by the service target population, become *coverage*, which in turn produces an improvement of the health condition or protection in the individuals served. These *outcomes* lead to an overall improvement of health status in the population, shown as *impact*. Traditional CEA, shown in the bottom left corner, has generally examined the extremes of the health system: inputs and impact.

The cost-coverage analysis presented here is an adaptation of the traditional CEA: It concentrates on the intermediate steps that lead to coverage, and it stops

Table 9.2
Recurrent Costs Related to Specific Stages of Production of Effective Coverage

STAGE	INPUTS
Effective Coverage: recurrent costs required to ensure that services are of sufficient quantity and quality	**Supervision** costs related to that intervention, including transportation costs (but excluding personnel costs) **Training** costs for review of skills (amortized where appropriate)
Utilization: recurrent costs required to ensure service delivery and contact with the target population	**Material** costs of direct services: drugs, vaccines, supplies, Village Health Worker information system, receipts from user fees **Development** costs for that intervention: raising awareness in the community, setting up village level committees (amortized where appropriate) **Monitoring** costs related to that intervention: monitoring, active outreach
Accessibility: recurrent costs of ensuring that resources are available and distributed to a location that is accessible to the population	**Transportation** recurrent costs for direct service delivery: fuel, repairs **Personnel** costs of village health workers (remuneration) for that intervention **Training** costs related to new skills added at village level
Availability: recurrent costs of resources required for services to be made available to the target population	**Infrastructure** recurrent costs for direct services: cold chain, health center maintenance **Material** (fixed) costs for direct services: administrative information system, office supplies **Logistics** costs related to maintaining supplies at the pharmacy (including buffer drug stocks) and to administering the community financing system
Structure: infrastructure and personnel provided by the government or external donors	**Personnel** costs for direct services for government-supplied manpower **Equipment** costs (amortized) **Transportation** costs of vehicles (amortized)

short of impact to focus on effective coverage. *Effective coverage* can be defined as the percentage of those people requiring a certain intervention who receive it in a correct and timely manner. Effective coverage is a proxy measure for effectiveness or impact.

Figure 9.2
Coverage with Childhood Immunizations
(Pahou PHC Project, July 1985-June 1986)

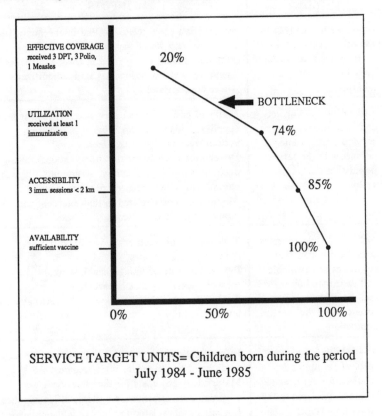

SERVICE TARGET UNITS= Children born during the period
July 1984 - June 1985

Using effective coverage as the endpoint has two advantages: It allows assessment of the distribution of benefits (equity), and it circumvents some of the complexities of measuring health status. In addition to health services, many variables, such as social, economic, and environmental factors, affect health outcomes and impact. These confounding variables make it difficult to reliably measure the impact a health program has on health status. However, it should be noted that using effective coverage as a proxy for improved health status assumes that the interventions are efficacious (i.e., that services given to the proper recipients and in the correct manner will have the desired result).

Specifying what goes on inside the "black box" between health resources and health outcomes is very important for determining possible management actions. Only by understanding how resources are currently being used will it be possible to see how to use them better. If program managers are to make decisions that will improve performance, they must be able to identify root causes of performance problems. Choosing appropriate management action requires knowledge of potential solutions and of the costs involved in implementing them. This cost-coverage model helps managers monitor coverage and analyze how they have used or could better use their resources to improve coverage.

The next two sections describe how coverage is measured (the coverage model) and how costs are allocated to achieve coverage (the cost model). Following these sections is description of the data needs and the analysis for this cost-coverage framework. The last section discusses some applications of the methodology.

THE COVERAGE MODEL

Achievement of coverage of those in need is dependent on factors of both supply and demand for the health intervention. Although the possible factors are numerous, they can be reflected in a limited number of determinants, representing, in effect, a hierarchy of conditions necessary for an individual to be covered.[5] The cost-coverage model examines how coverage is produced by examining four determinants of coverage:

1. *Availability of resources (service capacity)*: If services are to be provided, the resources required to produce these services must be present in sufficient quantities.

2. *Accessibility of services (spacial distribution)*: In order for the population to take advantage of service capacity, the services must be offered at a place and at a time convenient to those who need to use them.[6]

3. *Utilization of services (acceptance and contact)*: To achieve coverage with the services offered, the target population must actually use the services.

4. *Effective coverage with services (sufficient quantity and quality of services)*: The services delivered must be of a standard quality, and the target population must use them with proper timing and intensity.

This coverage model helps managers to define the coverage goals they are trying to achieve, to describe how the program is structured to achieve these goals, and to examine how well their target population is responding. Coverage with an intervention or a package of interventions can thus be measured using a series of quantifiable indicators, one for each determinant. These indicators are formulated as a percentage of the target population for which the conditions have been fulfilled. Table 9.1 shows the indicators used for measuring coverage with childhood immunizations in the Pahou PHC Project in Benin, West Africa for the period July 1985 through June 1986.

The values of the coverage indicators can be calculated and graphed to identify large differences between the individual coverage determinants. These differences represent the major bottlenecks for effective coverage, pointing out places for priority investigation and/or action. Using data from the same project, Figure 9.2 illustrates how graphing coverage curves based on the hierarchical model can point out where key problems lie. In this example, only 20 percent of the children are effectively covered with childhood immunizations. What the curve shows is that the problem is neither the availability of vaccine or the accessibility of the immunization sessions. Mothers were bringing their children to these sites to receive at least one immunization. However, as highlighted by the large drop between the percentage of utilization and percentage of effective coverage, the bottleneck is here. Possible reasons for this could be that mothers did not know that how many immunizations their children need or that mothers were not sufficiently warned about the possible side effects of the shots and never returned. The fact that mothers came at least once defines a different type of problem than if they never brought their children at all. Thus, assessing coverage in this manner focuses discussion, investigation, and action on the key problems (bottlenecks) in achieving high effective coverage.

This coverage determinant hierarchy has been used as a routine management tool in the Pahou PHC Project, in the national EPI/PHC program in Benin, and in the national EPI/PHC program in Guinea-Conakry.[7] Such coverage analysis can be carried out with routinely available data, with relatively simple analytical skills, and it has been found especially useful for identifying key service and management problems in attaining coverage.

THE COST MODEL

The companion cost model follows the same hierarchical framework as does the coverage model. It categorizes the costs of producing coverage (i.e., the costs of assuring resource availability, access to services, utilization, and effective coverage). The cost model is based on a multistage coverage "production" process and allocates costs to these stages. This cost model was originally developed to evaluate the costs of various strategies for achieving effective coverage. It has also been used[8] to asses (1) the relative contributions of the Beninese Ministry of Health, external donors, and user fee revenue to the various coverage determinant levels, and (2) the equity of coverage and financing of that coverage through user fees. Because the cost-coverage model was designed to assist managers in making decisions about resource needs, the costs included in the analysis should be those the manager has under his or her control. This limitation-of-scope model differs from traditional CEA, which

Table 9.3
Costs by Coverage Determinant for Childhood Immunizations
(Pahou PHC Project, July 1985-June 1986)

DETERMINANT	ZONE A	ZONE B	ZONE C
EFFECTIVE COVERAGE	$ 0	$ 124	$ 123
UTILIZATION	$ 145	$ 361	$ 382
ACCESSIBILITY	$ 0	$ 230	$ 89
AVAILABILITY	$ 43	$ 45	$ 52
STRUCTURE	$ 284	$ 621	$ 388
Number of target units	100	136	125

includes all costs. However, the cost-coverage model is designed to be used for managerial decisions, not societal-level decisions.

The cost model, as it was applied in Pahou, focused on costs covered by community financing revenue; other resources, such as personnel, were supplied by the Ministry of Health, and Pahou managers had no control over their magnitude. These costs were considered as the constraints under which the project managers must work, and were categorized as structure costs. They were not included in the total cost of achieving coverage. However, if such costs were under managerial control, they could easily be incorporated into the cost model.

The raison d'être of this cost-coverage framework for cost allocation is the calculation of *additional* costs related to each step in the achievement of coverage. Table 9.2 shows how costs of achieving coverage are built up from the bottom. The first category of costs, labeled *structure*, contains those fixed contributions by the government (e.g., salaries) and by external donors (e.g., amortized investment costs of buildings, transportation, and equipment). Following structure costs, the model accounts for the costs of *availability*,[9] those recurrent costs (beyond structure costs) that provide the health structure with the capacity to *offer* services. Availability costs include maintenance, administration, buffer drug stock, and cold chain costs. Without the resources to cover such costs, it would be difficult to ensure the potential for service delivery.

In order for the target population to take advantage of this service capacity, services must be offered at a time and a place convenient for them. Bringing the services out to the people (i.e., making them accessible) can require resources for outreach and decentralization (village-level personnel). This is

Table 9.4
Cost Variables and Data Sources (Pahou PHC Project)

COMMUNITY COST DATA	SOURCES OF INFORMATION
VHW remuneration	accounting records
fuel (service and supervision)	weekly programming calendars for # of visits per site, estimate of cost/km.
office supplies	accounting records
information system costs (Village Health Worker)	compile number of forms used, cost of paper
curative drugs and supplies	logistic records and treatment forms
preventive drugs and supplies	logistic records
maintenance and repairs	accounting records
cold chain costs	manufacturers'estimates
OTHER COST DATA	**SOURCES OF INFORMATION**
health worker salaries	Ministry of Health (average)
health center information system costs	market value for replacement
training costs	accounting records
equipment costs	accounting records
vaccine costs	logistics records; UNICEF prices

especially important for preventive care services, which are mainly provider-initiated. *Accessibility* costs have been set aside from availability costs so that differences in costs, for example, of a health center with an outreach program for immunizations and a health center without any outreach can be brought forth.

Once the services are physically accessible, contact must be made with the target population. This contact leads to *utilization*. Costs related to utilization include the costs of strategies to convince the target population to use accessible services (e.g., health education), as well as the variable costs of consumables, such as drugs and materials.

Effective coverage requires resources for ongoing training and close supervision to ensure continuity of care and a standard technical quality (e.g., that the right number of doses of vaccine are administered). The production of effective coverage requires resources additional to those of utilization, for training, supervision, and implementation of strategies to assure patient compliance.

Since each successive stage of production builds on the coverage determinant level below it, the magnitude of additional costs for each determinant will always be a function of the strategies used to maximize coverage achievement. Table 9.3 shows cost data by coverage determinant from three zones of the Pahou PHC Project. Each zone represents a different service delivery model: Zone A offers immunization at a fixed site (the health center) daily, Zone B has monthly outreach sessions in all hamlets, and Zone C has outreach sessions every six weeks in the major villages. Zones B and C use health center personnel and village-level workers. By calculating the additional costs of each step in the coverage hierarchy, one can see where resources are being expended and the effects they have on the overall achievement of coverage. The total cost of achieving coverage is then simply the sum of the "additional" costs at each stage of production: availability, accessibility, utilization, and effective coverage. Not that the costs associated with structure are not added into total costs. As noted earlier, these costs were covered by the Ministry of Health. Pahou managers had no control over them and therefore could not influence their effect on the delivery system.

DATA NEEDS AND ANALYSIS FOR THE COST-COVERAGE ANALYSIS

Data for Measuring Coverage

Assessing levels of coverage requires data that identify service target units, data on their access to services, data on their utilization of the services, and data on the technical quality of the services delivered. In the Pahou PHC Project, information on availability was compiled from logistics records. Access information was collected by mapping the project area and linking data on distances between hamlets and service delivery points with demographic information about the villages in the catchment area. Data for immunizations and growth monitoring were compiled from routine service records: cards for children under three years of age filed in a numbered family folders. Coverage data for other interventions were compiled from village-health-worker home-visit forms or through household surveys.

If the program has a reliable, up-to-date information system, much of coverage data can be compiled directly. Information on the number of services delivered can also be combined with information on the total number of target units for each service from a baseline census. However, for projects that do not

Table 9.5
Methods of Allocating Indirect Costs to Interventions

METHOD	DATA SOURCE	COSTS ALLOCATED
% effort personnel	work study data	health worker salaries, Village Health Worker remuneration
number kilometers traveled and cost/km.	planning calendar	transportation costs for supervision and outreach
% of floor space	health center floor plan	electricity costs, maintenance

have access to accurate data on their service target population, it may be necessary to do a household survey.

Data for Measuring Cost

Costs are defined as the monetary value of resources used to produce the service. Information on PHC service costs can be collected from a combination of routine accounting records, logbooks, logistics records, and work studies. Table 9.4 shows the sources of cost information for items covered by community user fee revenue and other sources from the Pahou PHC Project. Because accounting records are generally not broken down into service categories, planning for a cost-coverage analysis in advance can ensure costs are recorded in a manner that can be later compiled by function or intervention.

A PHC system produces many different types of services, causing many costs to be joint costs. In Pahou, allocation of joint costs among the specific interventions was conducted using an adaptation of a functional analysis.[10] This functional analysis methodology uses work study data and other methods to allocate costs to different health service *functions* or groups of activities. *Direct service functions* for the Pahou PHC Project were curative care, maternal care, well-baby care, immunizations, and environmental activities; *support service functions* included supervision, training, logistics/administration, surveillance/monitoring, and program development.

The functional analysis starts with directly allocating all costs that related only to a single function. Indirect costs (relating to more than a single function) are then allocated based on work studies (for personnel time), mileage, and distribution of floor space. Once all costs have been allocated to a single direct

Table 9.6
Distribution of the Costs per Intervention for Antenatal Care
(used in the Pahou PHC Project analysis)

personnel effort for antenatal care	ZA %	ZB %	ZC %
	(from work logging and work sampling)		
STRUCTURE			
equipment for antenatal	actual costs		
personnel (MC)	(cost MC) x (% intervention)		
electricity (MC)	(cost MC) x (% intervention)		
personnel SUP—MC	(cost MC) x (% intervention)		
personnel TRAIN—MC	(cost) x (% syllabus antenatal)		
personnel LOG—MC	(cost MC) x (% intervention)		
personnel MON—MC	(cost) x (# inter. monitored)		
personnel DEV—MC	(cost MC) x (% intervention)		
AVAILABILITY			
logistics/admin	none, because no charges		
infrastructure	(maintenance) x (% intervention)		
ACCESSIBILITY			
transportation—MC	(cost MC) x (% intervention)		
VHW—MC, SUP, TRA, LOG, DEV	(cost MC) x (% intervention)		
training: new activities	(cost) x (% syllabus antenatal)		
UTILIZATION			
drugs/vaccines: antenatal	actual cost		
information system forms	(cost) x (number of forms)		
DEV—MC	(cost) x (% intervention)		
EFFECTIVE COVERAGE			
SUP—MC	(cost) x (% intervention)		
refresher train: antenatal	(cost) x (% syllabus antenatal)		

MC = maternal care (antenatal, delivery, postnatal care)
VHW = village health worker
SUP = supervision
TRAIN = training
LOG = logistics
MON = monitoring/information systems
DEV = program development (planning, development of village committees, etc.)

Table 9.7
Comparison of Costs and Coverage with Childhood Immunizations among the Three Pahou PHC Project Zones: Percentage Coverage and Cumulative Cost per Child Covered at Each Determinant (June 1985-July 1986)

	ZONE A		ZONE B		ZONE C	
Effective Coverage	7%	$26.90	21%	$26.20	28%	$18.46
Utilization	58%	$ 3.25	83%	$ 5.62	76%	$ 5.50
Accessibility	72%	$ 0.59	93%	$ 2.18	88%	$ 1.28
Availability	100%	$ 0.43	100%	$ 0.45	100%	$ 0.42
Structure	$284		$621		$388	
# Children < 1	100		136		125	

or support service function, the costs of the support service functions are then allocated to the direct service functions. This is done based primarily on the basis of the distribution of personnel time among the various direct service functions. Table 9.5 presents the methods used for allocating the joint costs, such as personnel, transportation, and infrastructure. After the support service costs of each function have been added on, direct service costs are then distributed to the specific interventions being evaluated for coverage. In the case of immunizations that are administered at the same time as growth monitoring, work study data were used to determine the proportion of joint costs to be allocated to the immunization function. Allocating the appropriate portion of immunization costs to the childhood immunization intervention was based on the proportion of immunizations administered that were childhood immunizations: (#DPT + #Polio + #Measles + #BCG)/(#DPT + #Polio + #Measles + #BCG + #TT). Finally, the costs of the intervention are allocated to the various determinants of coverage, using the framework in Table 9.2. Table 9.6 presents an example of how the costs of maternal care related to antenatal care were calculated and allocated to the coverage determinants. All these calculations and allocations can be easily done in any spreadsheet software.

APPLICATIONS OF THE COST-COVERAGE MODEL

The cost-coverage framework can help health program managers in many ways. Managers can use it as a CEA tool to compare strategies for achieving coverage. They can use it to estimate changes in costs and coverage resulting

Figure 9.3
Immunizations, July 1985-June 1986
(Children Born July 1984-June 1985)

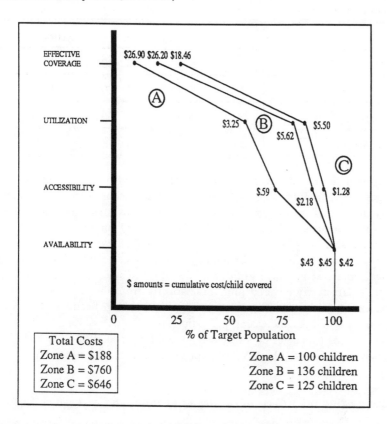

$ amounts = cumulative cost/child covered

	Total Costs	
Zone A = $188		Zone A = 100 children
Zone B = $760		Zone B = 136 children
Zone C = $646		Zone C = 125 children

from changes in service delivery strategies. They can use it to assess program sustainability by examining who is financing what aspects of coverage. Finally, can use it to assess equity of coverage and, if the program uses cross-subsidization of interventions, equity of financing.

Comparing Strategies for Achieving Coverage

In a more traditional CEA application, the cost-coverage framework can be used to compare various strategies for achieving coverage, either over time within the same area or between areas that have implemented different strategies. In the Pahou PHC Project, the three zones had differing strategies for immunizations. Zone A (population 3,500) provided immunizations daily,

Table 9.8
Costs and Coverage in Zone A (July 1985-June 1986) and Estimations under an Outreach Survey: Percentage Coverage and Total Cost per Coverage Determinant (Pahou PHC Project)

	7/85-6/86		new strategy	
Effective Coverage	7%	$ 0	40%	$100
Utilization	58%	$145	80%	$200
Accessibility	72%	$ 0	90%	$ 90
Availability	100%	$ 43	100%	$ 43

but only at the health center. Zones B and C held outreach sessions in the villages. In Zone B (population 3,000), outreach sessions were held monthly in 12 hamlets. In Zone C (population 4,000), these sessions were held every six weeks in 7 hamlets. The consequences for costs and for coverage can be seen in Table 9.7 and Figure 9.3. These data indicate that, even though Zone A has the lowest total costs, the community financing costs per child completely immunized are about equal to those of the other two zones. In fact, the costs per child effectively covered jump dramatically from the costs per child ever immunized (utilization). These data indicate that a village health worker (VHW) network is useful for increasing utilization and effective coverage. However, immunizations appear to be sufficiently sought after in Pahou, such that very frequent sessions and a high VHW/population ratio are not necessary.

Understanding the Effects of Strategies to Improve Coverage on Costs

The cost-coverage framework helps managers look for ways to improve coverage. The coverage analysis shows where the bottlenecks to coverage are occurring in the coverage determinant hierarchy. Managers can then assess the costs of strategies for improving coverage by estimating the effects. Taking the above example of coverage for immunizations shown in Figure 9.2 for Zone A of the Pahou PHC Project, we can see how this cost-coverage framework could be used. The Pahou PHC Project manager decided to change their strategy from one offering only immunizations at the health center to an outreach model. It was possible to see that coverage was low because accessibility was poor. Changes in strategy from immunizations available daily at the health center to outreach sessions also conducted in surrounding villages. Increases in estimated costs reflect transportation and increased costs of vaccines and training. Table 9.8 shows the costs and coverage rates in the first period, and estimations of changes: increasing access would have an effect on utilization and effective coverage, which in turn affect costs at those levels.

Looking at Where Efforts Are Being Placed

This cost-coverage framework can also be used to examine who is contributing to what aspects of coverage. Evaluations of costs and coverage for the various coverage determinants can be used to assess the distribution of funding sources throughout the coverage hierarchy. This assessment in Pahou revealed that community financing revenues contribute substantially to ensuring the accessibility of services and to paying the recurrent material costs of providing the care itself. Such an analysis can give indications about project sustainability: Examining where external donor inputs are being used can illuminate potential consequences of pulling out those resources when projects finish.

Examining Equity of Coverage and Equity of Financing

This same cost-coverage framework has been used to evaluate the equity of coverage with PHC interventions and the equity of financing under a curative-care user-fee structure. This equity analysis looks at coverage patterns (curves) for different socioeconomic groups and calculates the costs of coverage for each group. Costing coverage separately for each group permits reflection of their different coverage patterns.

In the Pahou PHC Project, the community financing system generates revenue from curative-care user fees, but provides preventive-care free of charge. The cost-coverage framework was used to assess whether the costs of preventive care coverage for lower socioeconomic groups were subsidized by the revenues generated from the use of curative care by higher socioeconomic groups.

CONCLUSIONS

The cost-coverage framework presented here is an alternative to the more traditional cost-effectiveness analysis models. It has been designed to assist managers in project implementation by increasing their understanding of how well they are reaching their target population, where their program falls short in achieving coverage, and how well they are using their resources to attain their desired coverage levels. This framework has been applied in a primary health care project in West Africa, and the coverage model has been used in many projects and national PHC programs in the region. However, the principles are equally valid for community-based health programs in the United States.

NOTES

1. K. Warner and B. Luce, *Cost Benefit and Cost Effectiveness Analysis for Health Care* (Ann Arbor, Mich.: Health Administration Press, 1982), 46.

2. K. Warner and B. Luce, *Cost Benefit and Cost Effectiveness Analysis for Health Care* (Ann Arbor, Mich.: Health Administration Press, 1982), 117-71.

3. See R. Parker, W. Reinke, A. Kielmann, C. DeSweemer, C. Taylor, and A. Srinivas Murphy, "Evaluation of Program Utilization and Cost-Effectiveness," in *Child and Maternal Health Services in Rural India: The Narangwal Experiment: Integrated Nutrition and Child Care*, vol. 1, edited by A. Kielmann, C. Taylor, C. DeSweemer, R. Parker, D. Chernichovsky, W. Reinke, I Uberoi, D. Kakar, N. Mashin, and R. Sarma. (Baltimore: Johns Hopkins University Press, 1983), Chap. 9; Danfa Project Team, *Danfa Comprehensive Rural Health and Family Planning Project, Final Report* University of California (September 1979); R. Grosse and J. DeVries, "Estimating the Costs and Effectiveness of Health Sector Policy Alternatives in Developing Countries," Health Planning and Economic Development Program, University of Michigan (January 1978); I. Sirageldin, V. Salkever, and R. Osborn, eds., *Evaluating Population Program: International Experience in Cost Effectiveness Analysis and Cost Benefit Analysis* (London: Croom Helm, 1983).

4. Funding for the Pahou PHC Project has been received from various sources over the ten years: 1981 to 1984—Ford Foundation (training, baseline survey, technical assistance), Unitarian Universalist Service Committee (reconstruction of health center, initial drug stocks, equipment); 1985 to 1989—Dutch Development Aid (research costs); 1990 to 1991—International Development Research Council of Canada (research and expansion to district level).

5. Such a coverage determinant model was first described by T. Tanahashi, "Health Service Coverage and its Evaluation," *Bulletin on the World Health Organization* 56, no. 2 (1978): 295-303. It was later developed into a routine monitoring framework in the Pahou PHC Project and is further described in R. Knippenberg, D. Levy-Bruhl, R. Osseni, K Drame, A Soucat, C. Debeugny, "The Bamako Initiative: Primary Health Care Experiences," *Children in the Tropics*, no. 184/185 (1990).

6. Accessibility could be defined in other terms, such as financial accessibility. The definition of accessibility is highly dependent on the situation in which the model is being applied. Access basically reflects an absence of constraints for the population when trying to make use of available services.

7. See R. Knippenberg, D. Levy-Bruhl, R. Osseni, K. Drame, A. Soucat, C. Debeugny, "The Bamako Initiative: PHC Experiences," *Children in the Tropics*, no. 184/5 (1990).

8. Lynne Miller (Franco), "Equity in the Context of Community Financing of Primary Health Care: Who Pays and Who Benefits?" (Sc.D. diss., Johns Hopkins University School of Hygiene and Public Health, 1989).

9. Availability costs, although conceptually similar to structure costs, have been set aside as a separate category here to represent those costs that are under the control of the "local" manager because these are usually not financed, or not sufficiently financed, by government budgets.

10. Department of International Health, School of Hygiene and Public Health, Johns Hopkins University, *The Functional Analysis of Health Needs and Services*, New Delhi: Asia Publishing House (1976).

10

The Case against Measuring "Cost-Effectiveness" in Nonprofits: Are We Barking up the Wrong Tree?

Jonathan B. Cook, *Support Centers of America*

When the planners invited me to speak at the National Workshop on Cost-Effectiveness in the Nonprofit Sector, their proposed title for my talk was "The Case against Cost-Effectiveness."

I was devastated. Where did I go wrong? After all these years of trying to make things work better, why didn't they ask me to make the case *for* cost-effectiveness?

After pleading with the planners, I got my role changed a bit. My revised assignment is to call into question the act of attempting to *measure* cost-effectiveness.

The premise of this chapter is that, in our current environment, nonprofits—including grantmakers to nonprofits—do so many other crucial things badly that conscientious attempts to measure cost-effectiveness are sure to be wasted.

Indeed, as evidenced by the behavior of nonprofits and their funders, no one even really wants meaningful measurement. A number of "deadly sins" of the well-intentioned people in the nonprofit sector erect substantial barriers to cost-effectiveness and its measurement. Most of those barriers cannot be surmounted within any one organization acting alone.

THE CASE AGAINST MEASURING "COST-EFFECTIVENESS"

Why is anyone interested in measuring cost-effectiveness at all? We do it *solely* to help decide which are the best practices and organizations in which to invest our time and money. Some things work better than others. Some organizations work better than others.

Unfortunately, huge amounts of time and money get spent on the wrong practices and organizations. Hence, the need for better information about what works and what doesn't. As shepherds of limited resources for good works, it is our job to keep track of our resources, our products, and our impacts. We will serve better if we understand what practices and organizations make the most difference and focus our resources on them. Right?

Maybe not—at least in the nonprofit world as we know it today. There is a case to be made that measuring cost-effectiveness is a waste of the very time and money it is intended to save. That case goes as follows:

> Don't bother—in any meaningful way—to measure cost-effectiveness. Evaluating your external results is never worth the effort and is usually a sham, performed for other reasons. If you bother, it won't matter. No one will do anything useful with the information you produce, no matter how good it is.
>
> If you discover you are wonderfully cost-effective, no one else will pay any attention anyway. If you discover you are relatively ineffective, you will hide that information and keep doing whatever you already do now.
>
> *Nobody* really cares about cost-effectiveness. Even if nonprofits *do* evaluate cost-effectiveness, are funding decisions really going to be made based on that analysis? Even if nonprofits *are* cost-effective, will policy makers make decisions that reflect that knowledge?
>
> Indeed, if you waste your time and money preparing all that information, you will in fact be *less* cost-effective because you will have foolishly wasted resources in preparing it.

Sadly, there is merit to this argument. The cards of the nonprofit sector *are* stacked against developing evidence that one method is more cost-effective than another—and are particularly stacked against developing and promulgating evidence that one *organization* is more cost-effective than another.

Advocates for the nonprofit sector—I count myself among them—point out that we do a lot of things right. We motivate; we bind wounds; we make important things happen. We are a special way for a society to take responsibility for itself.

In our efforts to perform conscientiously, we do use *some* cost-effectiveness information internally within our organizations. Our zeal for knowledge about how well we work is limited, but at least we don't squander a lot of money on it. We use information if it is easily available to us, and if it doesn't cost a lot relative to the uses we expect to make of it (which is actually somewhat cost-effective of us).

On the other hand, the reality regarding external uses of information about the cost-effectiveness of nonprofits is a disgrace. Outside the boundaries of a single nonprofit organization, information about cost-effectiveness is virtually never used objectively or competently.

Theoretically, the most important external use of such information is to enable effective allocation of resources to specific organizations and methods. But such factors as influence, loyalty, fund-raising skill, and fund-raising expenditure are much more significant determinants of where dollars go in our sector. For the most part, information about what works—or which organizations work—makes little or no difference in determining how resources are allocated by external sources to nonprofit organizations. So, why bother?

There is a strong case to be made that those attending this workshop on cost-effectiveness, and nearly everybody else, are barking up the wrong tree. Since measurement doesn't make a difference—the case goes—we should instead give priority to removing the barriers to achieving and measuring effective performance in the nonprofit sector. ("Effective performance" and "cost-effectiveness" are virtually synonymous. An organization cannot *perform* effectively without using its resources wisely.)

IDENTIFYING THE BARRIERS TO "COST-EFFECTIVENESS"

What could increase our cost-effectiveness if we did it with more efficiency, sounder logic, or greater wisdom? What are the weaknesses and problems that interfere with (1) nonprofit cost-effectiveness and (2) nonprofits' ability to make use of information about cost-effectiveness? What follows is an enumeration of some of the "cost-*ineffective*" practices and behaviors that I—and others I have asked—perceive as being most pervasive in our sector.

The list that follows is confined to the nonprofit sector itself. While there are business, government, and individual practices that affect our ability to perform cost-effectively, this chapter focuses on opportunities to influence cost-effectiveness that lie closer to home.

The remainder of the chapter organizes the possibilities for improvement within our sector in two classes, one internal (resource expenditure *within* nonprofits) and one external (resource allocation *to* nonprofits).

NONPROFITS AND HUMAN NATURE: BATTLING THE "DARK SIDE" (INTERNAL BARRIERS)

The dysfunctional characteristics of human beings the world over are at work in the nonprofit sector, too. Tribal instincts, self-interest, confused values, and myopia create illusions that distort our ability to judge what really matters. They fool us into erecting barriers that interfere with what, in fact, most of us ultimately care about: making the most of our lives.

Ego in the Nonprofit Context

We are an ego-dominated sector. In the business world, ego is restrained by necessity, such as the need to clothe one's children, or by investors' desire for financial gain. Those constraints play a less significant role, as well as a less measurable role, in our sector, thereby magnifying the role of ego factors in everything we do.

This factor has too many implications to cover here, so I will single out one: small business syndrome. People who want to "be their own boss" derive a lot of satisfaction from their independence. People who struggle to keep "their baby" alive derive a lot of satisfaction from their creation. But nonprofit leaders have no right to exhibit personal independence, create their own job security, or keep their organizations alive at the expense of more cost-effective service to their client base. Yet this is common.

Institutionalism: Territorial Beasts to the End

In watching nonprofit organizations, I am often reminded of the movie *Never Cry Wolf*, in which a scientist goes out to live in the wilds with the wolves. As he builds his relationships with the neighboring animals he is studying, a wolf seeks to demarcate its turf by urinating at its chosen boundaries. The scientist—being a mammal as well—figured out what the wolf was doing and urinated out boundaries as well!

Nonprofits urinate on their boundaries constantly.

It is literally in our genetic makeup to care first and foremost about our own territory and our own tribes. That's how our species survived to become civilized. Hence, when will nonprofits care about cost-effectiveness? Only when it can be used to help our "tribe."

Institutionalism is the consequence of this instinct. We work for the tribes of which we are a part—regardless of their relative cost-effectiveness. American universities and their devoted alumni's fund-raising efforts are a wonderful example. When universities were folding in the 1970s, did any go out of business because they discovered they weren't as cost-effective as the other organizations serving young adults? No. Other factors, such as number, age, and wealth of alumni, determined which universities survived.

Endowments

What a fascinating idea—*today's* organizations spending *today's* dollars on *tomorrow's* uses.

We will go to donors who love us and ask them if we can take a whole lot of their money that could be spent on something important now, and use it to guarantee the future of our organization—whether or not it stays at all effective.

We will ask them to provide us a guaranteed annual income, that will continue no matter how great the waste or inefficiency of our organization in the future.

What a tremendous scam! Universities with billion-dollar endowments routinely ask for more.

There is one exception to this knock on endowments. In the case of general-purpose private foundations and community foundations *tomorrow's* organizations use *today's* dollars on *tomorrow's* uses. They will make judgments in the context of future conditions when the money is expended. That's a big improvement. As long as the foundation does not use those dollars on itself, it keeps its sacred trust with the donor.

(This item relates to the question of how large an operating cushion is appropriate. See the section on grant-maker financial management skills below.)

Disproportionate Top Management Time Spent Chasing Money

How do the leaders of the nonprofit sector spend their time? Raising money, of course.

Who among the leaders of the nonprofit sector are judged effective? Those who succeed at raising money. Is there *any* other measure of the worth of a university president? It takes so much time and energy to get funding. As a consequence, the leaders of the organization cannot focus on the delivery of quality services. It's a sorry state.

Conversion of Public Dollars into Private Sinecures

Too often something goes wrong with the values of people who have risen to the top of nonprofit organizations, especially large ones. Having worked hard to rise to the top, humans expect others to pay us back. The hazing and the privileges of rank in fraternities and the military demonstrate the process. So also does the medical profession at its worst. After years of making no money, and then using their money to pay off their loans, once they get in the clear financially, many doctors see getting rich from human suffering as something they have earned.

Do nonprofits do the same when they get large and strong?

One famous university's difficulties with the federal government were recently well publicized. This particular university spends money on perks for its leaders and its donors. In fact, it spends lots of money this way. It even has a yacht.

It's bad enough that they tried to include it as legitimate overhead on federal research contracts. But why does any nonprofit—other than perhaps the yachting foundation—have a yacht?

Another example was my lunch at a foundation in New York. This particular foundation has its own lunchroom. Well, actually it has its own five-star restaurant, way up on top of its building. I had a superb meal; but more significantly, at that meal I was given the *best* service I ever got at any restaurant. Anywhere. There were waiters, a maitre d', busboys—and they did their jobs well.

Perhaps this was part of the foundation's interest in job creation.

And then there are the expensive dinners and $10,000 receptions at annual meetings of another nonprofit. Now, in this last example, these may be smart things for a money-seeking organization to do—they probably work. After going to these receptions, big donors then give them more money. Is that a good enough reason to spend charitable dollars this way?

Parenthetically, I should note that we are indebted to the sample organizations I have just mentioned for many important contributions. But do they provide their contributions cost-effectively? Would anyone even ask that question of them, or they of themselves, in a way designed to get a meaningful answer?

Fragmentation of Resources

Let me use my own field of endeavor—management assistance to nonprofits—as an example on this one. It's the one I know best, and the one I violate no confidences by discussing.

It is self-serving to say it, but I know the following statement is almost certainly true. The organization I work for can demonstrate, at a high level of reasonable assurance, that we produce twice as much product per dollar as do our competitors—or more—and that our quality is at least comparable and in some programs far superior.

No one ever asks. Not our grant-makers. Not our clients. No one has ever asked—with one exception that I will mention later.

The organization I work for is in a classic information-intensive business, where the costs of producing information are huge and the costs of using it over and over again are tiny. Our business *begs* for scale, but because it is so easy to hang out a shingle, many people do and the limited resources are fractured.

Other examples? Back where I come from, there are literally hundreds of Chesapeake Bay environmental organizations. The fragmentation of the African famine and AIDS organizations when those crises first became apparent are other sad testaments to this phenomenon. Can you get such organizations to merge? Nooo. Only if their money runs out will they consider it. The result: Money that could be spent to serve the client base better is directed to relatively cost-ineffective organizations and methods.

Management Skills

We've come a long way on this one; at least Peter Drucker says so. But there is still such a long way to go, especially in competitive analysis and strategic planning among like organizations. Let's all take credit for a job being done well and talk more about management another day -- which I look forward to doing with many of you.

No Common Measures of What We Do

Yes, we have learned that our "investors" don't care, that the quality of information (except for how good it appears visually and reads) is largely irrelevant to the funding process.

So what? Measuring cost-effectiveness is still our job, and we don't do it very well. What do we do instead? We do things that pretend to be measurement—we love to promulgate misleading measures. For example, it is so tempting to value volunteer hours in preposterous ways and neglect to mention associated costs.

One of my favorite misrepresentations was by the organization that liked to advertise that "$5 billion has been raised by organizations participating in our training programs." Think about it. It's preposterous—all you need is one representative from the Red Cross to attend your training to support that claim—but organizations do things like that all the time.

More importantly, I think we are afraid to measure. If we produce information and disseminate it, (1) our competitors will misuse it if they can, and (2) if their information is better than ours, they will make use of that to defeat us. Roughly, the logic goes as follows:

Grantmakers can't know we are cost-ineffective without getting information from our competitors as well, and that information is hard to get. Since we don't want to be compared to those other agencies for fear of what might happen, we better just shut up and sit tight.

Nonprofit competitors have good reason indeed to fear comparing data. The grant-makers could force us to the table if they could figure this out, but it would be nice in the interim to see us doing it voluntarily.

Each set of similar nonprofits must develop its own information standards. There are many different industries within this sector. Even though we are all called "nonprofit," different types of nonprofits are not even remotely the same from a measurement perspective. For example, comparing large-scale management training programs for nonprofits is easy. We do it all the time within the Support Center network, and we learn a lot about how to increase participation and satisfaction—and cut costs.   Service statistics and cost information from that program could be readily compared with those of training programs run by other organizations. We are not talking nuclear physics here.

The absence of common measures is an underlying reason for this workshop. If we had them, we would be able to measure our outputs and costs more usefully.   If there were meaningful common measures within each nonprofit industry, we could then approach the point where measuring cost-effectiveness would be cost-effective!

RESOURCE ALLOCATORS: THE GRANTMAKERS MUST DO THEIR JOB RIGHT FIRST (EXTERNAL BARRIERS)

When you talk cost-effectiveness, you have to talk of the resource allocators: the individuals, foundations, corporations, and government agencies that decide how discretionary resources will be allocated to the nonmarket activities of our society. The external process of allocating resources to organizations in the nonprofit sector is central to the cost-effectiveness of the whole shebang.

If the resource allocators don't do their job better, neither will the organizations using the resources (the incentives will be all wrong). If allocation *decisions* ignore cost-effectiveness, providers will be less likely to produce the information needed to make wiser decisions in the future.

Before running through my list of allegedly abhorrent grant-maker practices, I want to draw a parallel between resource allocators in the nonprofit sector and those in the business world. I think we could get nearly universal agreement that grant-makers are supposed to be the nonprofit equivalent of investment companies. Their job is to invest wisely in good causes.

Some may have a high-risk, venture capital mentality; others may want to invest conservatively in known quantities sure to produce a return. But they are all investment companies. What have foundations failed to learn from venture capital and investment companies? The sad truth is that nonprofit grant-makers are nearly universally incompetent at being investment companies. How could they be characterized in any other way? Imagine a commercial investment company that followed the practices of a typical grant-making organization:

- They would only invest in organizations that came to them—never in organizations that they sought out and tried to buy "stock" in.

- They would be predisposed to invest in organizations that made a good impression in brief meetings with other investment companies. They would learn about these impressions at monthly luncheons.

- They would be more likely to invest in organizations that put their name on a plaque than in ones that would return a profit.

- They would know little, if anything, about the cost-effectiveness of their fundees' competitors or, for that matter, even about the existence of their fundees' competitors. "Is there a competing organization that will give the client base more for this million dollars?" That question is never asked by most grant-makers.

- They would know little, if anything, about the long-range plans of their fundees or their fundees' competitors.

- When they finally found a winner, they would withdraw their funding after three years and start over someplace else.

And now to my external grant-maker list of barriers to cost-effectiveness in the nonprofit sector.

Lazy/Misguided Grant-Making Tactics

"One Grant per Agency per Year"

This restriction is generally reserved for small powerless agencies. If you don't believe me, look at the grant lists of some of the large foundations and look at the multiple grants to large nonprofits. But see what they tell you if you ask about grants for two separate great proposals from your small agency.

The worst effect of this foolish restriction is that it discourages nonprofits from merging—so they can each continue to get their one grant per year. This is no imaginary situation, by the way; I have been in it more than once.

The national environmental organizations have the same problem with direct mail donors. They can't merge because the direct mail donors give X amount in each gift. They'll give $10X$ to ten organizations or $1X$ to one organization. But never $10X$, or even $2X$, to one organization.

Project Support Rather than Effectiveness Support

At a recent Independent Sector conference, one of the sessions was about project funding versus general support funding. Both nonprofits and grant-makers present displayed an appalling lack of knowledge about what those words even mean. Non sequiturs were the norm, as more than half the people in the room didn't know the difference between "overhead" and "general support"! Some grant-makers felt that giving general support was the conceptual equivalent of failing to hold nonprofits accountable for specific results. It was a frightening meeting.

It doesn't have to be like that. One of the nice things to emerge from the grantmaking community was the study by Michael Seltzer and Michael Cunningham on "General Support vs. Project Support," funded by the Ford Foundation. The study laid out the logic of providing general support funding and alternative ways of thinking about this matter. We won't repeat that case here. This excellent study is a reminder that even though grant makers may not be "cost-effective" much of the time, they do care. (The study has been completely ignored, of course.)

In that study it was even reported that Peter Goldberg of the Prudential Foundation suggested giving *concurrent* general support grants to recipients of project grants. Bless his heart!

Here's a related idea for grant-makers who care: *Every* project grant should include an additional amount, perhaps 25 percent, for general support of the organization. And, no, that should not be in lieu of allowing the agency to account for some of its costs indirectly.

There are times when project funding is beneficial. One is when no organization has interests similar to the grant-maker (a rare occasion). Another is when the grant-maker wants to "buy" something that is already well within the scope and plans of the grantee. But, all in all, any grant-maker that "only funds projects" is harming the organizations that are trying to do good works in our society.

Requests for Proposals (RFPs)

I hate them. Through an RFP, many different organizations are invited to write proposals, even though only one will get the money. Many will be rejected based on a perceived lack of qualifications regardless of what they write. In addition, RFPs are expensive to respond to. Not infrequently, more money is spent by the organizations applying than is given away by the grant-maker.

RFWs (requests for waste) would be a better name for these little monsters.

Think of the organizations that live at the RFP trough: When do you think they work hardest and longest? When they are serving their clients? Nooo.

Requests for qualifications (RFQs) make a lot more sense and are an easy substitute. All organizations should be maintaining information on their knowledge, experience, and productivity anyway. An RFQ just says "show us what you have; show us what you can do." *After* a small number of top candidates are quickly chosen based on capability and cost, negotiations on product should be conducted.

The RFQ process increases the likelihood that the funder will get the best provider for its need, unclouded by who spends the most time seeking the inside track on upcoming procurements or writes the best dissertations showing their "understanding of the problem." Truly cost-effective organizations will rarely be willing to spend their time this way. They will have to know they are "wired" before they will spend precious resources responding to RFPs.

Application Procedures

Done in small doses, application procedures are fine. But beware of application procedures that (1) require more than a minimal amount of information that will be used for tracking purposes within the grant-maker, or (2) request information that the grantee does not need for its own management.

Government agencies have developed such specialized business procedures that now only certain nonprofits can even do business with them. Experience with the procedures, and with the unique process requirements of the government agency itself, becomes a distinct competitive advantage that makes it difficult for other organizations, not part of the inner circle, to even present their case to the agency. To play with the government, you often have to be willing to spend lots of time and money on RFPs and reports, rather than on clients. One result: Efficient providers do less business with the government.

Just think! Some private grant-makers appear to aspire to learn to be like the government.

Waiting for Proposals (WFPs)

These are the worst FPs of all. The amount of foundation and corporate funding an organization receives is heavily dependent on the amount of money and time, especially chief executive time, the organization spends on fund raising. Leaders that should be driven to examine every nook and cranny to figure out how to make their programs more effective instead examine the nooks and crannies of grant-maker styles, preferences, and personnel.

It is difficult indeed to be lean and mean and also to be successful at fund raising. One of the best positioned new organizations in the United States has spent most of the money it was given publicizing itself. Is that bad? It's hard to be sure. Perhaps this is a legitimate start-up strategy that effectively conditions the donors that will support it now and later.

Meanwhile, alternate investments are out there all the time, but are ignored because they don't come to the door—while the grant-maker WFPs.

Is failing to come to the door a fault of the missing nonprofits, who may well be spending money on clients instead of fund raising and publicity? Is it a sign of poor management? Perhaps it is, since the act of going to the right doors is a prerequisite of major financial success in the nonprofit sector. But this condition only exists because of grant-maker practices, so which is the chicken and which is the egg?

Lack of Strategic Planning

Fads and responsiveness to the wrong factors are a problem in any human endeavor, but the risks are heightened when you make no plans at all.

For all their talk about nonprofits and good management, grant-makers don't plan. They do *think* they plan. They make lists of areas of interest and call that planning, and in some small way it is. But it is not the kind of planning we need from them. We need a whole different understanding of strategy and strategic behavior on the part of our "investment companies." Today, overloaded as they are by the systems they have constructed, they are not willing to do the work it would take.

Lack of Focus Area Strategies

For the most part, today, it can be said with assurance that grant-makers have no coherent logic for the choices they make *within* their fields of interest. If they give to day care, they give to "good" day care organizations and programs, with "good" leaders, that come in the door.

The logic for this approach is that the foundation grant-makers do not want to dictate to the field. They want to hear from the field what works. That's a poor excuse for not taking the time to learn about the organizations and strategies that work best in a specific field of interest.

Occasionally, grant-makers, on their own initiative, have joined with other funders to intervene in specific nonprofit industries in certain ways and with specific focus area strategies in mind. There have been significant examples of this in the housing, economic development, and nonprofit-sector research fields. Foundation staff themselves usually think of the ideas that receive the benefits of these consortium strategies. (You'd think the rest of us might have an occasional good big idea, too.)

Funding Newness

Foundations and some corporations love to make grants for "up to three years" and for "innovative" projects. Somewhere along the line, grant-makers confused the concepts of venture capital and innovation. To an investment company, newness and oldness, per se, are not the key when investing in cost-effectiveness—which is the only sensible goal for an investor. It is possible, and often profitable, to invest to make existing organizations stronger. (Venture capitalists call these "mezzanine" grants.)

Not Funding Cost-Effectiveness

Both grant-makers and providers cannot make the best use of information about cost-effectiveness unless we can compare it with comparable information from other organizations that might use the same resources. (Comparative cost-effectiveness needs to be judged both for actual *and potential* results and costs.)

Amazingly, concern for cost-effectiveness at an operant level—*who does the most with the least*—seems virtually nonexistent among grant-makers. I think I am not exaggerating when I say that in twenty years of working with grant-makers, I have been asked about comparative cost-effectiveness only once. After I formulated an answer and sent it in, the grant-maker complained that we had been uncomplimentary to a competitor (an organization in which the wife of one of her bosses played a special role).

Incompetence at Financial Analysis and Financial Management

Incompetence is a strong word, and I have now used it twice I realize, but it is not an exaggeration when used to describe the financial management knowledge of institutional grant-makers today. Grant-makers have expectations about the financial management of nonprofits that are either incorrect or deliberately unfair.

Take indirect costing. Nonprofits are taught—Support Centers teach them—to use methods of indirect costing as a way of simplifying (and, in most cases, making far more accurate) financial statements. It also saves them accounting time and money and makes them more auditable. (Overhead costs are costs, common to a number of programs, that are pooled and indirectly allocated in a batch, rather than directly allocated to each program line by line.)

But most grant-makers do not understand that the indirect ratios and the reporting conventions of indirect costing are *meaningless* outside of the context of each organization. Removed from an understanding of that context, many grant-makers confidently give a doubly meaningless refrain—"we only fund programs, we don't fund overhead"—not realizing that it is perfectly possible to characterize every indirect cost as direct if one wants to spend additional accounting time and money to do so.

Thus encouraged to report directly the costs that should be accounted for indirectly, total costs wind up *higher*, but the ratio reported to the donor winds up looking lower. The result? Happy donors, spending more money to get less result, but with a nice low overhead rate to make them feel good.

Despite the efforts of the Council on Foundations and Stanford Research Institute, grant-makers, virtually 100 percent of them, still do not have an accurate understanding of the basics of the techniques for understanding what things "cost." (Nonprofits don't either.) "We won't pay overhead," of course, means that someone else must. Accounting for costs directly does not justify them; it only heaps additional sins upon the funder demanding such an expensive and foolish practice.

Organizations with extravagant costs, whether accounted for directly or indirectly, should not be funded by *anyone*. You can know what is extravagant only if you (1) examine specific costs or (2) examine total products compared with total costs of competing organizations within subsectors.

Another of grant-makers' financial management sins is their confusion about the concept of a financial cushion. How much money can a nonprofit have on hand and be eligible for financial support? One of their favorite questions (to small organizations) is: "You have a little money in the bank, so why are you asking for more support from us?" For years, in fact, some United Ways treated *any* opening fund balances as income that agencies were required to apply in order to project a zero balance at the end of the upcoming year. Talk about trying to drive an agency out of business!

The flip side of this is what they tell the large, prestigious organizations: "You have a huge endowment, much of which you could have directed toward operating costs but you choose to it put away for later years since you don't need it now. My, what good management you have!"

Failure to Understand the Economy of the Sector

By definition, the nonprofit sector is a "nonmarket" economy. The principles of Adam Smith's marketplace don't work here—at least not the same way or nearly as well.

Producers and consumers in our sector do *not* participate in an arm's length exchange that serves to control cost and quality. In a marketplace, consumers provide the resources. In a nonmarketplace, third-party funders provide the key resources. The dynamics are different. The top leader of nonmarket organizations must spend their time and talent pleasing the market that matters—their funders, the providers of capital for their programs.

Competition for consumer dollars—the heart of the free market resource allocation process—does not have the same power in a nonmarket economy. Indeed, many nonmarket functions are actively diminished by competition. Job banks and public libraries are examples of functions that show greatly increased cost and greatly decreased effectiveness the more providers there are. So, too, for subsidized "infrastructure" organizations, such as information centers and management training providers.

Other levers must be used to help nonmarket organizations be effective. These can include

- Better information systems that help us gain understanding of what practices and organizations work best

- Disclosure

- Comparison with information from similar providers elsewhere

- Decentralization and diversity that allow competition of ideas

- Good management within and among like organizations

When nonprofits compete, many funders are tempted to let the marketplace "sort it out." All that does is assure that the most economically successful providers will prosper and that true non-market services will not be sustainable. And which grant applicant is most economically viable in a nonmarket economy? Whoever is successful at raising funds from other donors, of course.

GIVING CREDIT WHERE CREDIT IS DUE

My assessment of the resource allocators is a harsh one. If this assessment seems too harsh, it may be because it fails to emphasize that the provider organizations could get and disseminate better information on their own. But, in fact, providers can't or don't. They won't provide information about cost-effectiveness until the resource allocators change their behaviors about this information and its role in their decisions.

I have had many opportunities to see institutional grant-makers at work. Like the rest of us in this sector, they work hard, and they care deeply. They carry a lot of burdens—not the least of which is that every day, they live with the unrealistic barrage of expectations from all the people who seek the money they control.

Nevertheless, they are barking up the wrong tree. They must begin to insist upon the creation and the disclosure of comparable forms of measurement among comparable nonprofits. And they must use that information. This is a realistic and attainable goal.

WE CAN CONQUER THE DARK SIDE

In concluding, I'd like to tell a story about someone who did conquer the dark side.

One of the unsung heroes in the nonprofit sector is an *information* hero. In the late 1970s, the National Society of Fund Raising Executives hired Wilson (Bill) Levis to conduct a study of fund-raising costs. Doing the study proved impossible, however. The ways information was being reported by nonprofits were too disparate to allow comparability. In particular, almost every state government had different reporting requirements for nonprofits, so that it was impossible to compare information reported in one state with that reported in another. And, of course, the forms asked for the same information to be reported in different ways—an accounting and financial reporting nightmare.

The President's Commission on Private Philanthropy and Public Good (the Filer Commission) got wind of the problem—with help from Levis—and suggested standardized reporting as part of the solution. Aided by that credibility enhancer, Levis created the Uniform Annual Report Project. He orchestrated, virtually single-handedly, a campaign to get all the state governments and the U.S. Internal Revenue Service to agree to use the same report form. The project got off the ground to a universal greeting from a chorus of well-wishers: "It's a great idea, but it can't be done."

Three years later, thirty five of thirty nine states with separate reporting requirements had agreed to use IRS Form 990 as their basic information report.

This sole action—doing the "impossible" in an information area—has saved the nonprofit sector literally tens of millions of dollars in the last decade. We can do the same within our own fields. Of course, there are times when meaningful measurement is difficult or impossible. But there are many other times when it is relative child's play.

Should we quantify? Should we compare? Yes, we should.

One way to chip away at the problems I have enumerated here is to chip away at them with good information. Better information about cost-effectiveness *will* help break down other barriers.

In sum, the thesis of the workshop is valid after all. Comparable forms of measurement are needed among comparable nonprofits and should be demanded by boards, funders, and other leaders—as well as by all of us in the field.

APPENDIX A: Nonprofits' Deadly Sins: Things the Resource Spenders Do to Prevent Cost-Effectiveness

1. Ego in the nonprofit context

2. Institutionalism: Territorial beasts to the end

3. Endowments

4. Disproportionate top management time spent chasing money

5. Conversion of public dollars into private sinecures

6. Fragmentation of resources

7. Management skills

8. No common measures of what we produce

APPENDIX B: Grantmakers' Deadly Sins: Things the Resource Allocators Do to Prevent Cost-Effectiveness

1. Lazy/misguided grantmaking tactics, e.g.,
   a. "One grant per agency per year."
   b. Project support, rather than effectiveness support
   c. Requests for Proposals (RFPs)
   d. Application procedures

2. Waiting for Proposals (WFPs)

3. Lack of strategic planning

4. Lack of focus area strategies

5. Funding newness

6. Failure to fund comparative cost-effectiveness

7. Incompetence at financial analysis and financial management

8. Failure to understand the economy of the sector

Index

About the Editor and Contributors

Jorge Baanante, a native to Peru, currently works as a Field Representative for the Pan American Development Foundation. During his twelve years of experience in economic development and financing, Mr. Baanante has held qualified positions related to planning, financing, and evaluating development projects both internationally and domestically.

Fred Balderston is currently Professor of Business Administration at the Walter A. Haas School of Business Administration at the University of California at Berkeley. He has served as Vice President of Business and Finance and Vice President of Planning and Analysis for the University of California and has been a member of numerous professional organizations.

Margaret Bowman, the Country Director for TechnoServe/Nigeria, has worked extensively in the areas of policy research and analysis. Ms. Bowman initiated and solely designed and managed a new start-up program for TechnoServe, a nonprofit international development agency promoting enterprise development, in Lagos, Nigeria. Other experiences include Consultant for the ARIES Project at Harvard Institute for Research and Development, Project Analyst for ACCION International's credit program, and a Graduate Internship with the United Nations Office for Development and International Economic Cooperation.

Jonathan B. Cook is the National Executive Director of the Support Centers of America, a network of nonprofit management assistance centers located in twelve cities around the United States. Mr. Cook is a recognized authority on the nonprofit sector and on the management of nonprofit organizations. Before working for Support Centers, he was Executive Director of Public Interest Management Associates, where he had a major role in the development of the first nonprofit management and accounting assistance center. In 1991, he was honored as a "Washingtonian of the Year" by *Washingtonian* magazine and received the Prudential Foundation's Leadership Award.

Thomas Dichter currently works for the Aga Khan Foundation in Geneva, Switzerland, as the Program Officer of Institutional Development. Dr. Dichter has had various professional experiences, including Peace Corps Volunteer, Program Evaluator for McBer & Co. in Boston, Director of Evaluation and Development of the New Jersey Education Consortium, consulting ethnographer for the World Bank, owner of a cabinetmaking business, and Director of Special Programs for TechnoServe Inc. In 1980, Dr. Dichter accepted a position as Director of the Peace Corps program in the Yemen Arab Republic for which he received an Outstanding Performance Award from Peace Corps/Washington.

Anne B. Evans is the Administrator of the National Gallery of Art and is a member of its seven-member executive officer group. Ms. Evans was a Vice President with the MAC Group, an international general management consulting firm. She also conducted a study of the motion picture production business for WNET/13, the public television station in New York, and worked in newspaper and photographic publicity for the Smithsonian Institution's Division of Performing Arts in Washington.

Lynne Miller Franco is an Associate Scientist in the University Research Corporation/Center for Human Services International Development Group. She is a member of the organization's Quality Assurance Project staff and has been involved in a number of projects, including operations research studies in Niger. She developed and manages the Quality Assurance Information Base, which serves as the archive for data from over 200 research studies, and has expertise in community financing, monitoring and evaluation, and curriculum development.

Eric Halperin is the Assistant to the Chief Financial Officer at The Nature Conservancy, an international conservation organization. Mr. Halperin was a member of the professional auditing staff of Ernst & Whinney and held positions with the Renewable Energy Institute, a Washington, D.C. based nonprofit public policy organization, and Power Towers, the first wind-power developer in the state of California.

Steven Londner is currently working as Association Director for the Cornell Cooperative Extension in Schoharie County, New York. In addition to this work, Mr. Londner does consultancy work for TechnoServe, Inc., where he held the position of Program Officer for the Africa Division for five years. He has worked as an Agricultural Economist and Agriculturalist for the U.S. Agency for International Development in Somalia, as a Country Representative for the American Friends Service Committee in Ethiopia, and as an Irrigation Agronomist for the Ethiopian Ministry of Agriculture.

Heather Johnston Nicholson is Director of the Girls Incorporated National Resource Center in Indianapolis, Indiana. Dr. Nicholson has been with Girls Incorporated (formerly Girls Clubs of America) for ten years, first as Senior Research Associate and then as Acting Director of the Center. Prior to joining Girls Incorporated, Dr. Nicholson taught Political Science and Public Management at Indiana/Purdue University, designed policy games for adults as Humanities/Science Fellow of the Indiana Humanities Council, and was Assistant Professor of Political Science at Purdue University.

Debbie Cohen Pine is a management consultant to nonprofit organizations. Ms. Pine has worked as a Senior Associate for Strategic Decisions Group, a management consulting firm in California, and as a Marketing/Computer Consultant for Hewlitt-Packard Company. Ms. Pine was Founder and Executive Director of the Alumni Consulting Team (ACT), a volunteer organization that encourages Stanford Business School alumni to serve as pro bono consultants for nonprofit organizations. She was also a Founder and Charter Committee Member of The Peninsula Community Foundation's Catalyst Fund, which provides seed capital to nonprofit initiatives that serve people on the San Francisco Peninsula.

Peter Reiling is currently the Africa Region Representative, located in Accra, Ghana, for TechnoServe. Prior to this position in Ghana, Mr. Reiling held other positions for TechnoServe, including the Director of the Replication and Dissemination Department, and served three years as a Senior Program Officer for the Africa Division. He has worked with a variety of agencies in his twelve-year career in international development, including the World Bank, USAID, Oxfam-America, and the Peace Corps.

Gerald L. Schmaedick is the Vice President for Research and Development of TechnoServe, Inc. He was promoted to this position after serving for twelve years as TechnoServe's Vice President for Latin America. Mr. Schmaedick has served as consultant to the World Bank, U.S. Agency for International Development, and the InterAmerican Development Bank on assignments in Asia, Africa, and Latin America. He was contributing author to *The World Food Budget—1970* (U.S. Dept. of Agriculture, 1965) and *An Evaluation of the Food for Peace Program* (U.S. Agency for International Development, 1972). He is an economist and a member of the American Economics Association and the American Agricultural Economics Association.

William B. Stason is Vice President of Health Economics Research, Inc. From 1984 until 1990 he was Director of the Department of Veterans Affairs' Northeast Health Services Research and Development Field Program. He is also a lecturer on the faculties of the Harvard School of Public Health and Harvard Medical School. He is an expert in technology assessment and cost-effectiveness analysis and was awarded the American Medical Writers' Association Book Award for his book (with Milton Weinstein) entitled *Hypertension: A Policy Perspective* (Harvard University Press, 1976). Dr. Stason has served as a consultant on health policy and technology assessment to numerous government agencies including the Agency for Health Policy and Research, the Blue Cross and Blue Shield Association, and private industry.

Rebecca Paxton Stewart currently works as for the Research and Development Department of Technoserve, providing computer graphic and textual support. Ms. Stewart has worked as a Placement Director for the Katherine Gibbs School in Connecticut, has owned a bookkeeping and accounting service.

Milton C. Weinstein has an extensive background in the academic field. He is currently the Director for the Center for Policy and Education at the Harvard AIDS Institute, the Henry J. Kaiser Professor of Health Policy and Management at the Harvard School of Public Health, the Director of Doctoral Programs for the Department of Health Policy and Management at the Harvard School of Public Health, and a member of the editorial board for the publication *Medical Decision Making*. Dr. Weinstein has produced numerous publications for medical and economic journals, and has done consulting for many corporations.

Faedra Lazar Weiss is Research Assistant at the Girls Incorporated National Resource Center in Indianapolis. Ms. Weiss is an experienced researcher, writer, and editor and has been involved in the writing of numerous papers on Girls Incorporated projects, including the Preventing Adolescent Pregnancy project. Ms. Weiss is the primary author of *Truth, Trust and Technology: New Research on Preventing Adolescent Pregnancy*.

Leslie A. Williams is currently Vice President of Conscious Solutions Group, Inc. in Seattle, Washington. At the time of the writing of this chapter, Ms. Williams was a financial analyst at The Nature Conservancy.